WALKING THE
EXECUTIVE
PLANK

WALKING THE EXECUTIVE PLANK

Why management firings happen —
and how to reduce them

CHESTER BURGER

VNR VAN NOSTRAND REINHOLD COMPANY
NEW YORK   CINCINNATI   TORONTO   LONDON   MELBOURNE

Van Nostrand Reinhold Company Regional Offices:
New York Cincinnati Chicago Millbrae Dallas

Van Nostrand Reinhold Company International Offices:
London Toronto Melbourne

Manufactured in the United States of America

Published by Van Nostrand Reinhold Company
450 West 33rd Street, New York, N.Y. 10001

Published simultaneously in Canada by Van Nostrand Reinhold Ltd.

15 14 13 12 11 10 9 8 7 6 5 4 3 2 1

TO ELISABETH

There Are No Words

Survival in the Executive Jungle
Executives Under Fire
Executive Etiquette

Introduction

The free-and-easy firing of corporate executives is primarily, but not exclusively, a phenomenon of the United States industrial scene. Nowhere else in the western world are executive dismissals so quickly considered, so smoothly executed, and performed so frequently.

This book takes a thorough look at the whole unpleasant business of executive firing—why it happens and when it happens. What causes it, and how to avoid it. How many firings are murder, and how many are suicide. I also question whether you are the executioner or merely the attending physician whose job it is to certify the death of the incumbent.

Many senior corporate executives in the nation's largest corporations have discussed their experiences with me in connection with the preparation of this book. Many of these men are named in the book itself, usually without their corporate identifications. Others, including personal friends, kindly reviewed portions of the manuscript and gave me their helpful suggestions. These include James M. Freeman and Conrad Pologe, American Telephone & Telegraph Company; Alvin Vogel, The Securance Corporation; Frank Steele, National Urban League, Inc.; Emmett Nathan, Western Electric Company; Sheldon B. Satin, Throckmorton-Satin Associates; Lloyd N. Newman, Manning, Selvage & Lee, Inc.; Eli Jaffe, Mt. Sinai School of Medicine, New York; Donald Kirsch, Wall Street Consultants, Inc.; Sol Zatt, Sol Zatt & Company; Bernard F. Agnelli, Western Union Corporation; Samuel P. Bates, Minnesota Mining and Manufacturing Company; Nancy L. Lane, The Chase Manhattan Bank, N.A.; Terence A. McCarthy, New York Stock Exchange, and John Harvey, Metropolitan Life Insurance Company.

To those who told me their experiences and their observations, I am deeply grateful. My gratitude especially extends to the many who could not allow their names to be used because of possible embarrassment in their corporate posts.

My thanks also to my assistant, Miss Brenda Dawson, for her preparation of the manuscript, and to my editor, Michael J. Hamilton, who suggested the idea in the first place.

CHESTER BURGER

Chester Burger & Company, Inc.
New York, New York
September, 1972

Contents

WALKING THE
EXECUTIVE
PLANK

1

Playing the Game You Can't Win

YOU DIDN'T SLEEP WELL ALL NIGHT. Now you've awakened feeling slightly edgy and irritable. You don't relish going to the office. In the back of your mind lurks the barely-suppressed hope that the trainmen on your commuter special will go on strike today. Then you'd have a legitimate excuse to stay home.

Why? What are you afraid of? What are you trying to avoid?

Are you worried about getting fired?

Not at all. Quite the contrary. You're worried and

angry and upset because this afternoon, you're going to have to fire Don Lombardi, your young assistant manager. It won't be a very nice day.

But it's all been decided and agreed upon. Your boss has approved the action. The personnel chief has initialed the termination papers. When you arrive at your office, someone from the personnel department will be there with all the necessary forms in a brown envelope, including the man's final payroll check. The usual check list will be included to remind you to pick up his credit cards before handing over his money.

So there's no escaping your duty. You can't stall any longer. You can't give him another chance. You're just going to have to call him in, give him the word, and then face the music.

You feel slightly dirty and greatly embarrassed by the whole procedure. You have in your mind a picture of his return home from the office that night, the scene where his wife greets him at the door of his house and he tells her, "Dear, we're in trouble. I've been fired. I'm out of a job."

And you'll be the cause of it. No wonder you feel guilty, angry at him for "making" you do it.

No doubt about it: firing an employee, particularly an executive, is Number One on the list of unwanted management responsibilities. Very few bosses like to do it. Most bosses absolutely detest it.

Look at it this way: when you fire an executive, you accomplish only two good things, but at least three bad ones. On the accomplishment side: you presumably improve the work of your department by ridding yourself of an unsatisfactory performer. And you give yourself a reputation as a tough, non-nonsense S.O.B. (In many companies, that's a highly desirable reputation to have.) On the negative side, you may frighten the rest of your staff.

You earn the victim's lifelong enmity, and you damage your reputation as a fair-minded boss. (Everyone wants to believe the victim's story of why it happened, not your version —even if you were free to tell it.)

The odds are hardly in your favor. So why do it? Because you must. Because you really have no choice. Because the man's failure to perform his job is creating problems for the rest of your department and above all, making waves for you.

Or so you've decided, anyhow.

You may indeed be right. But even if it's too late to do anything about today's victim, it's not to late to look ahead and consider what can be done to avoid the next crop of dismissals.

Not just because they're a disaster to the men terminated, and an embarrassment to you, but because the social cost is so high. One can detect beneath the bubbling surface of corporate America some indications that in the future, corporations may feel (and therefore be) less free to terminate employees or executives. There are barely discernable indications that public opinion (and therefore the public's elected representatives) may be beginning to look less kindly and more critically at corporations that dismiss employees and executives for any reason at all, short of malfeasance or gross breach of discipline. I even seem to detect faint mumbles and rumbles in certain segments of public opinion that perhaps a corporation, when it hires an employee, should assume virtually a lifetime responsibility for that man.

From my perspective, in the heart of competitive private enterprise America, this seems an appalling thought. I have visions of hordes of incompetents sitting around offices busily doing nothing, meanwhile dragging down the corporation to their own mediocre level.

Walking the Executive Plank

Maybe I'm wrong. After all, as you'll see in Chapter V, the Japanese have a setup like that right now, and their no-fire system seems to work no worse than our fire-at-will concept. It makes you wonder.

Maybe, however, dismissals from management will increase because of the economic recession, instead of being curtailed by social pressures.

If so, they deserve our closer look. Can we reduce their number and strengthen the corporation? How many dismissals really can't be avoided? How often is personal pique and antagonism responsible, rather than failure to perform?

Once upon a time, not so long ago, I believed that if you were fired you probably were the victim of injustice. All of my working lifetime, that's exactly what I had seen happen again and again. I had seen friends, close friends, on whose neck the corporate executioner's axe had fallen. And I felt great sympathy for my friends. Before it happened, there were always rumors circulating around the office that so-and-so would be the next to go. The action rarely came as a complete surprise. There was conversation over the water cooler and in the men's room about what was in store for Don Lombardi. And, of course, the rumors eventually reached the man. I used to think this was terrible; the torment he was being put through. Don (or the current victim) would always try some desperate last minute moves to strengthen his position with his boss. He might work longer hours on into the night or come in early in the morning beyond all reason, or look frantically busy. But it never seemed to make any difference; the blow fell anyway.

My earlier experiences suggested that most dismissals were arbitrary, caused almost entirely by personality conflicts. I no longer believe that, although I remain convinced that the most common cause for dismissal, deserved or otherwise, is inability to get along with the boss.

"The boss will sometimes overlook faults among his managers and supervisors," Paul Osgood, a high-ranking executive comments, "just as parents choose to overlook some of their children's shortcomings, because the boss really considers the shortcomings as partly his own fault. But bosses won't overlook one thing: insubordination. The minute a staff man gets insubordinate to the boss, he's had it! Forget it. He's through, and the boss will toss him out like an empty beer can."

Let me translate into plain English the term "inability to get along with the boss." It can mean refusal to follow your instructions. It can mean refusal to recognize your status. Or it can mean a simple thing like just plain forgetting you're the boss.

And when your junior managers refuse or forget to do any of these things, you can be quite certain that they're beginning to make problems for themselves. If they irritate you, they make it more difficult for you to evaluate their work with a cool professionalism. By their actions and attitudes, they've started on the trail that may eventuate in their dismissal.

It's difficult for any of us to terminate someone else's employment. Few of us are so hardened that compassion and sympathy fail to affect us. But I personally don't feel such sentiments in every case. My dividing line is drawn between the manager who tried his honest best but failed, and on the other hand, the executive who simply didn't try very hard. The fellow who enjoyed exercising his hostilities on me; the fellow who spent his time politicking instead of performing, or covering his wandering trail with memos instead of results, deserves little sympathy from me, and he gets even less.

2
Where the Trouble Begins

IN THE BEGINNING WAS THE HIRING. Often, the firing starts at the moment when you hire the wrong man for the job.

What happened to Erman W. Stott (that's not his real name) illustrates that very clearly. Erman was a high official in an independent agency of the Federal government. He had a good reputation in the industry which his agency watched. And in time, a leading company in that industry offered him the post of chief executive. He was delighted; the pay was only slightly better, but how else does a top

Where the Trouble Begins

government official find job security when the National Administration may change at the next election? So Erman left Washington and took his corporate job. He continued doing exactly the things he had done so well on Constitution Avenue. He went to meetings; called many of his own; attended endless business and trade association luncheons; and mediated the disputes of his corporate managers. He was an expert mediator. Soon, an office joke developed on the executive floor: "If two people are in complete agreement, Erman will find a way for them to compromise and save face."

But his techniques that had worked so well in the government failed Erman in his corporation, because the needs of the two jobs differed. In government, often, a mediator is needed to harmonize conflicting interests. But the primary job of a corporation president is to keep his company moving ahead. In most company situations, dynamism rather than stand-pattism is what's needed at the top.

Erman became a troubled man. He couldn't understand why corporate environment didn't respond to his "leadership" as his government environment had responded. The company lawyers were already considering Chapter XI (of the Federal Bankruptcy Act) before Erman solved the major part of the problem by submitting his resignation to the Board of Directors.

Yet the fault wasn't really Erman's. He not only did the best he could, but he followed exactly the same management style that had brought him the corporate job offer originally. The error, obviously, had been made by the Board of Directors when they picked the wrong man for the job.

And in an insurance company, I know a fellow who quit only three months after he had taken the job. When he completed his training on "Estate Planning," he suddenly realized that what his employer really wanted from him had been concealed in bureaucratic double-talk. The company didn't really want him to be a "counselor in family estate planning" as they had said and as he had believed. They wanted him to *sell life insurance*. This wasn't what he wanted. This botch-up was due to management misrepresentation; it led to employee failure.

These cases—and they are quite typical—were minor disasters from the management viewpoint. Both could have been avoided.

The two firings essentially stemmed from the same cause. Erman Stott was the wrong man for the job. Management got in Stott exactly the qualities it wanted, but it wanted the wrong set of qualities for the post of chief executive. And in the case of the insurance man, the company needed a salesman, but when they described the job as an estate planner and consultant, they hired a man who had those qualities—but who didn't want to sell life insurance.

So the solution for this type of problem is quite clear: we've got to perceive accurately the qualities necessary for success in a particular job.

You can minimize your chances of selecting the wrong person if you can precisely describe the job you want done. In one Denver corporation, the practice is to set up a job description like a contract. The man reads it and signs it before he's hired, so he knows exactly what he'll be expected to do. If it isn't what he wants, it's not too late for him to back away from the job.

This system also tells a man exactly how his performance will be evaluated. Claude Oglesby, the Arapahoe County man who installed this system, tells me that new executives seem to know when they're not performing according to their contract. "They may not admit it, but subconsciously, they know whether they're measuring up," he says. "I have had cases where a man walked in and told me this wasn't the right company for him and he was leaving." That's another firing avoided.

Sometimes our own personality blind spots cause a mismatch. Managers sometimes unconsciously select a man because he resembles themselves in personality, even though those characteristics aren't what the job requires. In one case, for instance, a good friend of mine picked a tactful fellow for a post that required someone who was devious, aggressive and rough. He didn't recognize the mismatch. I suppose the only way you can avoid this trap is to think through the personality characteristics as well as the experience you want for a particular job.

In another case I know of, a man was performing the wrong job and working very hard at it. It occurred in a clothing manufacturing company whose security chief was coping with a plague of thefts that had caused $1 million in inventory losses. When the clothing company fired the security official, he protested that he had done an excellent job of protecting the factory and its inventory; he regularly inspected the guard patrol not less than five times daily!

"Yes," said the vice president for manufacturing, "but that wasn't your job. Your job was to stop thefts. And here are the figures. Stealing has increased since you took over, despite that fact that we've upped your budget for plant protection."

The dismissed security chief was immediately escorted off the company property by a member of his own guard staff. The chief had a gun permit and a .38 Special under his belt, so the company wasn't taking any chances with his temper.

The best single method I know to avoid such hiring errors is to introduce the element of deliberate delay into your recruitment. Don't make hasty decisions. Pick out likely candidates long before you'll need them. Get acquainted with them over a period of time. Go to lunch with them occasionally, and even correspond with them occasionally.

"When I finally got hired in one job," says James F. Fox, a New York public relations executive, "my new employers already had acquired a great deal of psychological as well as factual information about me. They had been talking with me over a period of many months. They had arranged for different people to meet me under different circumstances. Early in the morning for breakfast. Or for a drink after five o'clock one afternoon. They invited me to sit in a department meeting to observe how I handled myself. I'm sure they also watched to see whether I really wanted the job. The passage of time often unearths potential or actual problems and difficulties that would not reveal themselves in a couple of hurried interviews."

The protracted search and selection process in choosing an executive compares to that of wooing, becoming engaged and finally marrying a girl. You really ought to know your choice well before you decide to marry her. I think this comparison is apt because the factor of "chemistry" is so important.

There's nothing mystical about the meaning of that word "chemistry" so commonly used in management circles. It refers to the quality of personal relationships among the executives. As I've written in my previous books*, I think you can define "chemistry" even more precisely than that. My definition is, how you handle the boss. Bad chemistry is more likely to mean hostile attitudes than failure to perform.

*Survival in the Executive Jungle, (Macmillan, 1964) and Executives Under Fire, (Macmillan, 1967).

"If a manager is surly to me," comments a tough old boss in South Bend, "if he gives indications of being hard to work with and doesn't show the ability to handle people right, that's all I need to make up my mind against him. You damn well know when a man's attitude isn't right. You feel it. And I trust my feelings. I won't hire a man like that."

Indications of attitude problems often show themselves in a preliminary interview. They're more likely to show during a series of interviews over a protracted period of time.

Let's consider first the attitudes that are likely to cause problems. The trouble areas are not a man's individuality, his social or political outlook. Those matters are his private business. What we are concerned with is solely his ability to do the job. If, not so latently, he shows profound hostility to any form of authority, the likelihood is that he'll be unable to take direction from his supervisor.

Or if he's a rigid personality, self-righteous and arrogant in manner, you'll have problems. He may be a man who's masking his insecurities with the armor of absolute certainty. How will you be able to suggest improvements to such a man when he'll construe every criticism as a blow to his fragile ego? Such a type will frequently cause trouble as soon as he's hired.

A management consultant friend suggests another type of manager to avoid: the one with frankly-stated prejudices. He recalls one young man who was applying for a management job. "The fellow told me he didn't like smart aleck college graduates," my friend said. "He said he preferred someone who had worked in a shop for several years, over a well-trained young engineer. Sometimes that's o.k., but anybody who generalizes his pet likes and dislikes will bring trouble later on and I'd just as soon avoid it. You put a man like this in a management slot, and you're just asking for trouble."

Of course, bias against college graduates is rather unusual these days; prejudice against young blacks in management posts is more common, and at this writing, the idea of women in management's sacred ranks is deeply resisted by "male chauvinists." I don't think you'll find any management candidates without some prejudices, but I would suggest that if a man has the fervor and ardor of a crusader against one group or another, he's not likely to function as an effective manager.

Can you detect these traits early enough to avoid hiring a built-in failure? Not always. But sometimes.

When you check his references by phone, how does his former employer speak of him? It doesn't bother me especially if a man had been fired previously; most everyone has been at one time or another. I'm much more interested in the reason why. If he didn't get along with his last boss, I try to learn why. From the candidate's description, and from the former boss's own version you hear on the telephone, you can sometimes assess whether it was a clash of two angry and aggressive personalities, or whether it was, as the candidate insists, a situation where the prime villain was his boss alone.

Observe whether the candidate is considerate toward you. If he shows signs now of hostility, even before he has the job, there isn't much likelihood he'll suddenly prove amenable to his associates and staff later on.

Does he show up late for appointments? Does he treat the receptionist and your secretary with courtesy or with arrogant indifference? When he speaks of his former employer, does he describe the relationship with some reasonable degree of objectivity or instead does he speak with malice?

Do his comments have a quality of objectivity? Is he able to stand back detachedly, look at what happened and appraise it with reasonable self-honesty? Or does not-so-repressed anger ooze from his pores and a hard glint develop in his eye, when he speaks about his former boss? If this latter is the case, he's giving you a clue that he's likely to recreate the same situation if he comes to work for you. Maybe you can avoid firing him later by avoiding hiring him now.

Neither you nor I will ever eliminate all hiring errors. Nor will the assorted magician's bag of psychological tests that are supposed to do so. But your careful judgment can reduce the number of mistakes.

Firing is a painful experience for any man. It's also a loss to the company that is forced to do it. How much better to take prudent steps to eliminate the problem before it starts. "The past is prologue," said Shakespeare. If a man's life history up to the day you employ him is a history of conflicts, hostilities and failures, what are the odds that under your beneficent management, he'll suddenly change his life pattern?

Better put your bets instead on The New York Mets. At least, there you'll have some chance to win.

3
Nobody Wants to Do It

LIKE THE LITTLE SCHNAUZER DOG WHO WAS TAUGHT TO WHISTLE "DIXIE," THE SURPRISING THING ABOUT EXECUTIVE FIRINGS IS THAT THEY HAPPEN AT ALL. A friend of mine who heads a large corporation in the air conditioning industry told me, "I don't think I'd fire one of my executives unless I found him in bed with my wife. Nothing short of that." It's hardly what you expect to hear from a tough corporate boss.

The bigger the corporation, the less likely you'll feel free to fire one of your junior managers. It just isn't done.

It's bad corporate manners, almost as bad as slurping your coffee at the luncheon table in the executive dining room. If a manager or executive isn't performing satisfactorily, the company usually tries to find a quiet spot for him, some place where he can operate safely without danger of harm to the company.

Take the case of George Hamelfarb, a 58 year old purchasing executive in an oil company. At the time I was retained to do a management study in his department, George's daily pattern of action consisted of going to lunch at 12 o'clock and coming back at three, closing the door, and going to sleep.

This wasn't my opinion. It was a fact. George had an important job in the company. But he wasn't performing. And he was giving only half a day to his employer. He had a drinking problem.

I discussed the problem frankly with his boss, and was surprised by the response I got. "It's really no skin off my nose if George stays," he told me. "We can find a place for him somewhere or just leave him where he is. He's not doing any harm. I've decided to let him stay on for another two years and then give him an early retirement." Since I hadn't been hired to evaluate personnel, I let the matter drop right there. Good 'ol George is still on the job, 50% of each day, anyway.

The problem drinker benefits most often from the corporate reluctance to fire a manager. Even though it may be common knowledge around the office that the man is chronically intoxicated; even though it may be commonly recognized that he's severely in need of psychiatric help, many managements prefer to ignore the problem for as long as possible.

"If it got to the point where it just couldn't be postponed any longer," an editorial executive told me, "I suppose

Walking the Executive Plank

I'd call the man in and say, 'It's come to my attention that people are saying. . .'

"Of course the usual pattern is for the man to deny it. Usually, the more he denies it, the surer I am that he's got a problem. That's when I begin watching more closely and trying to build a case. But I hate to do it. Maybe we all feel that we might someday turn into alcoholics too. So we keep him on."

Ben Kimball is another man who should have been fired and wasn't. He worked for one of the large temporary employment services. He had been there for 19 years. For a long time, his boss had wanted to fire Ben. But the "gentlemen's agreement" in management prevented it. Repeatedly, his boss went to the president to discuss the Kimball case. "I've got a pensioner on my hands," his boss would plead. "I'm saddled with him. I'm not getting my job done. I'm not even being fair to Ben because, in effect, by keeping him, I'm telling him he's doing an acceptable job. It isn't true. Not only that, but I'm depriving some qualified younger person of a promotion to his spot."

Make good sense? Of course it did. But the boss wouldn't go along with it. "Is Kimball really hurting us badly? Is he doing the company irreparable harm?" the top man asked. Ben's boss could hardly say yes to such leading questions, so Ben Kimball is still on the job and now he has 21 years of seniority.

I know of another incident that occurred in a machine tool manufacturing company in the southwest. Mike Snowden, a section chief, had fallen into difficulties with his boss and his job was on the line. Apparently the boss and the division manager had been discussing Mike's possible dismissal when Mike walked in unexpectedly. As he entered through the open doorway, he overheard the two bosses talking about him. "Is Snowden really any good?" Mike replied defiantly and without being asked, "Mr. Hicks, I am damn good. I'll show you."

Believe it or not, it worked. On the basis of that incident, Snowden lasted another three and a half years on the job before he finally fell to the corporate firing squad. The division manager had been impressed by Mike's game spirit and it became one more reason or excuse to avoid letting him go for another three and a half years.

A vice-president for personnel in a commercial finance company, Jeff English, gave me a report of an account executive who, he said, should have been fired 15 or 16 years ago. But nobody ever made a decision to fire him. "We know within the first year if a manager isn't doing his job," Jeff insisted. "We know that in our business, our clients won't complain if they're getting poor service. They need our financing and they don't want to endanger their business relationships with us. But despite that, we've been getting rumbles about this account executive for years. Several of our clients let it be known they'd like their account transferred to another executive. That's pretty extreme. It's never happened to anyone else in this place, as far as I know. Usually it's a matter of total indifference to our clients as to who services their account.

"So this man probably should have been dropped within the first year. But what do we do now? I'm stuck with a 17-year mistake. My judgment is to fire him this afternoon and not let another day go by. But the president won't let me."

"If you had been his boss, would the president have let you fire him after he had served only five years?" I asked. "After 10 years? Where do you draw the invisible dividing line?"

Jeff replied, "By my standards, length of service should have nothing to do with it. An account executive's job isn't a political appointment. The guy isn't covered by a union contract with the United Executives and Management Wheels of America, AFL-CIO. If he isn't doing the job we need doing, he should be thrown out. But in our company, there's an unwritten rule. I suppose you could say that when you get your 10-year service pin, you're safe for the rest of your working life."

Hugh Herrick, a department head in a textile manufacturing firm, made a similar discovery. He recalled the time when he first had joined his company and had been assigned to a veteran supervisor.

"It took me only three days," Hugh told me, "to recognize that this man not only was not a supervisor, but his personality offended people. He failed to do his job satisfactorily. It even became a question for me what he was actually doing with his time all day."

I asked Hugh why he was so positive that the man was an unsatisfactory supervisor.

"He'd issue *dicta*," Hugh replied. "You know what that means? Just plain orders. 'Because I say so.' No consulting anybody. Just 'Do as I tell you.' For instance, I remember one memo he put out, 'Starting tomorrow, everyone will be at his desk by 9:00 a.m. If not, you'll have to stay two minutes after 5 o'clock for every minute you were late in the morning.' Isn't that ridiculous? So I raised the issue with the next-level boss in the chain of command.

" 'We can't fire this man,' the boss told me. 'After all, he's got nine years with the company.'

"I said, 'I don't understand. What does nine years give him? Is there a tenure contract?' "

"That's the way we do things in this company," was the reply. So the man stayed. He's still there.

Why not fire these men? A corporate division head

gave me one excuse, "When you fire a man, in effect you're saying that the man who hired him was a fool."

Of course that's nonsense. When you fire a manager, you're simply saying he hasn't done his job competently, and there's no suitable place to transfer him. To suggest that the man who originally hired him is a fool is rather far-fetched. It implies that the employment officer should have had 100% foolproof, guaranteed-perfect judgment. If such foolproof pre-indications exist, they haven't yet been discovered by psychologists or personnel interviewers.

It's not too difficult to fall into this pattern of never firing anyone. You don't have to do anything. You just do nothing. For year after year, you let things stay as they are. By the time it's become obvious that the inept or inadequate executive is impeding progress, you hope you'll no longer be his boss or responsible for his (in)activity. Then the other guy will have the problem, and presumably he'll do nothing either.

Or you may decide the misfit should be fired, but do nothing about it. In some companies, after you've made the decision to fire, it's a tribal custom to begin collecting evidence to justify your decision.

In most large companies, the decision to fire is not made by one individual. It's usually made by a group, including the man's supervisor, and perhaps the supervisor's supervisor. It's discussed with the personnel department and sometimes with other staff people as well. It's rarely an impulsive decision. Evidence is needed.

You begin to assemble a dossier and keep it in a locked file. Henceforth, you enter every transgression, major and minor. The man's arrival and departure times will be duly noted. Any minor irregularities, or even questions, about his expense account will be noted. Any failures to deliver work due, even lateness by a single day, will be commented upon in writing. Gradually, you'll build the file. The evidence must be overwhelming. When you feel your case is strong enough, you want no argument from anyone in the corporate hierarchy that you're acting arbitrarily.

But even a thick dossier doesn't always produce action. A business associate in a giant conglomerate described the phenomenon: "People in a large corporation are reluctant to take action. They've already decided the person is going to be fired. They've decided it intellectually, that is. But for whatever reason, they can't bring themselves to do anything about it. So the dossier, instead of becoming a device to justify action, becomes a device that is used to justify inaction; there's never quite enough evidence in the dossier to prove that the man deserves to get tossed out. In my company, an employee can go right to the president if he feels he's being unjustly treated, so the supervisor simply doesn't want to take chances with being overruled by the higher officials."

It all comes down to the fact that firing is an unpleasant business. Managers avoid it whenever they possibly can, to the detriment of their companies. Sometimes you get the feeling that everybody in management is primarily concerned with protecting everybody else.

Since mistakes are human, every company has its share of men in the wrong jobs, incompetents, and the like. But their superiors are preoccupied with covering up what has happened before. They hope this protection will buy for them equal protection from their colleagues if they make the wrong hiring decision. In the Army, the so-called (actually non-existent) West Point Protective Association performs the same function: "Protect my career today and I'll protect yours tomorrow."

Nobody Wants to Do It

In company after company, I've heard and seen similar cases.

When you hear stories like this over and over again, you begin to wonder about the highly-touted efficiency of corporate America. You begin to wonder whether management has the courage or firmness or good judgment to fire men promptly when they ought to be fired. If you have the courage to dismiss people when they ought to be dismissed, you will be recognized as a rare bird. You may soon find yourself receiving invitations to address your local management association as a man of distinction.

4

What Choice Do You Really Have?

VERY OFTEN, DISMISSING AN EXECUTIVE IS A MOST IMPRACTICAL "SOLUTION" TO YOUR MANAGEMENT PROBLEMS. So companies often search for alternatives to firing. The general agent of a life insurance company explained why he tries to avoid dismissals:

"When you fire someone, you're saying to him in effect, 'You can't do the job, so I'm going out to the labor pool and get somebody who can.' Some experts say that it costs a family of four $10,400 just to live at the poverty-level in New York City. Right away, I figure, $10,400 approximates the commission one of my salesmen makes by selling one million dollars of Ordinary Life Insurance.

"So, if you work for me and you're selling only *half* a million dollars worth of insurance, you're certainly not doing your job. On that basis, I could call the 73 men in my agency, and say to 33 of them, You're fired. That's based on last month's figures.

"That presupposes there is a labor pool out there somewhere from which I can draw qualified people to replace them. But you know that if I called the State Employment Service and said, 'Send me 33 million-dollar producers,' they'd hang up on me. It just isn't realistic. Such people aren't available.

"So I'm left with only one practical alternative: to do better with the men I've already got. I can't transfer them to other jobs, because in an insurance agency, there's no place to transfer them.

In reality, you often just make the most of a bad situation rather than fire poor performers and try to replace them with better-qualified people."

In many companies, and particularly in larger companies, however, transfer to other posts sometimes is possible. Clearly, American corporate managers consider transfer less often than they should.

On the subject of transfers and demotions, we've gotten ourselves into a bind. In our corporate society, you customarily move up every few years during your career to bigger salaries, bigger responsibilities and more impressive titles, until finally, one day, you find yourself out of your job. Not retired but fired. (Do a majority of U.S. executives eventually retire voluntarily or are they forced out in one way or another? It would be interesting to find out. I've never seen statistics, but my observations suggests that dismissals are more frequent than voluntary retirements.)

Walking the Executive Plank

As you ascended the corporate ladder, your salary rose to the upper levels of the stratosphere. As a vice-president, you may have been making $30,000 to $50,000 a year. As a fired ex-vice-president, suddenly, you're making zero.

Does this make sense? Why drop from $30,000 annually to zero? Why not perhaps to $15,000 or $20,000? If you're qualified to hold a lesser post within the company, why not? It's so logical that you almost wonder why it practically never happens.

The answer is that nobody can enthuse about his own demotion. The man loses status in the presence of his colleagues. It is an embarrassment. It is construed as failure. It causes such personal humiliation for the victim that he'd rather work elsewhere, anywhere, even remain unemployed, than to stay with his company in a lesser position and take orders from those who once reported to him.

It's human. One can understand it. But look at both the loss to the man and to the company. From his viewpoint (particularly if he's an older man), almost positively his next job will pay less than his last one. Even if he's hired into a post at the same level as the job he lost, his pay is likely to be less, because now he's a newcomer to his new employer. So clearly, he suffers.

And the company? Consider that the reason he had been promoted into Job B was that he had done well in Job A. Management can't put him back into Job A without humiliating him totally. But is there a Job C where he might perform effectively?

Downward mobility, semi-voluntary demotion if you will, rarely happens in our corporate life today. I know of only one or two corporations that permit it or practice it.

But downward mobility ought to be considered more

What Choice Do You Really Have?

often than it is, as an alternative to dismissal. There are three factors I would consider before recommending it in a specific situation:

First, does a job exist which the man is qualified to perform? Make-work, a phony job created as a sop to his injured pride, is wrong. Such "jobs" fool no one; they damage the company and eventually they destroy the self-respect of the man who holds one. A real post with work that needs to be done is another matter entirely.

Second, does the man really want to continue working? Has his motivation been either destroyed or seriously damaged? Are you firing him because he lacks ability to do the particular job and not because he lacks effort?

Third, how does the man himself feel about it? If you have satisfied yourself on the first two points, perhaps downward mobility should be discussed directly with him. Absolute candor is the only possible way you can handle this situation if you have any realistic hope of retaining him in the company. There is no room for circumlocutions in your conversation. First, he must be told that his performance in his present job has been unsatisfactory, and that he is being relieved of it immediately. However, since the company values his ability and experience, it wants to try to find a way to utilize him elsewhere rather than terminate him.

The post that's open, let's say as Supervisor of Technical Purchasing, is at a lower-level than the job he's just had. Its salary is less. If he were to accept it, there's simply no way of disguising to his friends and associates that it's a demotion. No doubt about it. It would be an embarrassment.

On the other hand, the company believes he could do that job very well, and he might want to consider it in preference to something on the outside. You express to him he'll decide to accept it, but you can understand ay prefer not to.

idering the unquestioned shock of the notice of termination from his present position, you can hardly expect the poor man to decide instantly whether to leave or to stay, or to express gratitude for your offer. It therefore might be judicious to give him several weeks to make up his mind. His termination is effective immediately, but if he decides the lower post you're offering him is better than anything he can find on the outside, you will welcome him back with no loss of seniority or benefits, and he can be assured of being treated with full dignity and respect. At that point the decision becomes his to make.

A friend of mine actually confronted this dilemma a number of years ago, and the way he handled himself increased my estimation of his high character.

Unfairly accused of responsibility for a corporate failure over which he had no control, my friend was summarily stripped of his officer's title but left in the same job, suddenly bereft of the corporate status that he had earned in a decade of outstanding service.

It was almost ten years later before the corporation corrected its error. They then restored the vice-presidential title to my friend. The president's action was decent, generous, deserved, and long overdue. After it had happened, I asked my friend to tell me his story in frank detail.

"First of all," he revealed to me, "you must understand that ten years ago, I was never given any choice. I was called in, and criticized by my boss, as you well know. Then he told me my vice-presidential title was being taken away.

"Nothing further was discussed with me, nor was I given any choice. I'm certain the boss expected me to quit. In almost eleven years with the company, I had never before heard of an officer losing his title. It was absolutely unprecedented. In an outfit like ours, if they're not happy with a guy, they fire him. That's par for this industry. I'm positive the president thought I would just get up and walk out for good.

"But since he didn't ask me to decide anything, I figured I needed a week or two to catch my breath, and think things through for myself.

"I had to size up my options realistically. The first fact was quite obvious—there was no future for me in this company. It would take all I had just to stay in the spot they left me in, even without a V.P. title.

"I asked myself if I could do as well or better elsewhere. I tried to size up the opportunities in other companies that might be open to me. I looked at my age—I would have been 50 on January 10th of that year—and putting it bluntly, I decided I would be better off if I could stay right where I was.

"Once I made my decision, I decided to live with it enthusiastically. It seemed to me there was a great peril if I sulked, or if I tried to give the boss as little work as possible. I thought they had been totally unfair to me, but I was not going to make things worse for myself by going around with a long face.

"You can be sure I never thought this day would come when I'd have my old title back. I suppose it was a one-in-a-million shot. I must have done something right."

To this day, I don't know why the president hadn't simply fired my friend ten years ago. Not that he deserved it. The presiden't action was totally unjust. But because my friend really wanted the job, title or no title, high status or low status, he hung on. In the end, the company and he both benefitted because an executive firing had been aborted.

There's another alternative to firing a man, namely, getting him to quit voluntarily. Not by driving him up the walls with frustration, but by arranging to have him lured away from your own company with a better job offer elsewhere. The twist is that he'll never know you were responsible for generating the offer.

The way it's done is to retain the services of an executive recruiter to find another job for him. Your company pays the recruiter's fee. The executive himself pays nothing. The company that gets him pays nothing.

The recruiter will eventually track down a suitably attractive opening and contact your man with the lure of a better opportunity. When your man bites at the bait and gets the other job, you will act the part of the surprised and rejected suitor when he notifies you of his imminent departure. Under certain circumstances, "out-placing" (the trade name for this management pirouette) can be less expensive than keeping an unproductive manager on your payroll for indefinite periods of time.

In this *pas de deux* you arrange a testimonial dinner in honor of old Joe as your final corporate act. The theme of the after-dinner speeches is We're-sorry-to-see-ol'-Joe-go.

Some of his associates really are.

They don't know how it really happened. And old Joe never will either.

Another alternative to the routine firing is dismissal for cause. The distinction between the two is clearly drawn in most companies: a routine dismissal is for unsatisfactory performance. A dismissal for cause takes place when larceny, gross insubordination, a major impropriety, or something of equal seriousness, has occurred. In a dismissal for cause, all normal payments are denied (except for accrued vacation pay).

When a corporation follows a generous policy of

severance payments, sometimes a discontented supervisor begins to look at them with longing and desire. In a Los Angeles aircraft supply company, Harry Dell told me of a young manager in his department who had become increasingly tart-tongued and insubordinate. His acrid manner was beginning to be noticed by the rest of the management group, but somehow, Harry hadn't been sensitive to it. The manager's peers wondered what he was up to, but as the pattern developed, they soon saw it quite clearly. Everyone did, in fact, except Harry.

Finally, when Harry didn't respond to his provocations, the young manager sent him an abusive inter-office memo. It was so full of invective that there were simply no grounds for delay or further discussion; he had to go. Harry now knew he'd have to fire the man. But his instinct told him something more: the pattern of insubordination, climaxed by the inter-office memo, was so out-of-keeping with the man's ordinarily cool personality that maybe he was trying to provoke his own dismissal in order to collect severance pay. "So I decided to call his bluff," Harry said. "I fired him for cause. That means that under our company policies, he was entitled to not a penny of severance pay.

"And sure enough," Harry went on, "wouldn't you know that he came into my office complaining not about his dismissal but about our denial of severance pay. And sure enough too, he turned up working for one of our competitors on Monday morning. It was a put-up job."

Even when it seems clear that an executive must be fired for poor performance, some companies still add one last step, a committee appointed for the purpose of reviewing proposed executive dismissals. Dismissals are not permitted without review and approval by the panel.

The three-man group reviews a man's entire personnel file. To minimize personal pique as a cause for dismissal, the panel considers only material that appears in the written file. If the man's supervisor is unwilling to sign his name to the allegations and stand behind them, they won't be considered.

A wise observer of the corporate scene once commented, "If the boss wants to make one of his staff look bad, he's got everything on his side." So if "bad chemistry" is the root cause of the proposed firing, the committee believes they'll detect it and prevent an injustice from being done. I once sat in on one of these groups and if they're all like the one I observed, they're certain to reduce the number of dismissals. When they refuse to sanction a firing, the company usually transfers the executive to another spot. And since the man was never informed originally that his firing was being considered, his boss, whose recommendation has now been rejected, has not lost face.

Some corporations do follow policies which seem to minimize or eliminate the problem of dismissals. One interesting approach is used in the Western Electric Company, the manufacturing and supply unit of the Bell System, and a company I regard (from personal observation) as one of the best-managed organizations in America.

Western Electric's policy stems from its need to train broad-gauge managers for top positions. So it transfers its best men and most promising managers from one post to another. The transfer might be to similar work in another plant, or to another department in the same plant. It might be a higher level of responsibility in the same type of work a man is now doing. Or it might be totally different work, and will need to be preceded by intensive retraining. A personnel man might be offered, for instance, accounting duties.

This sort of rotation, of course, can operate success

What Choice Do You Really Have?

fully only in large corporations. And often it brings real hardships to the family of the executive being rotated. How many times during a childhood can a youngster be transferred from one school system to another without educational or even psychological damage? How many times can a wife rebuild her circle of acquaintances and neighbors, or find employment for herself in a city to which her husband has been newly transferred? The problems are real, and the damage is often real, despite the company's best efforts to minimize them.

The net effect of such transfers, I am convinced, is to stimulate able men to peak performance, and to keep them stimulated by new and increasingly important (and difficult) challenges as they move up within the company. Perhaps this policy is one reason why Western Electric very rarely loses its best men to boredom and job fatigue as happens so often in other companies.

I'd be hard put to estimate whether the benefits are greater to the company or to the employee. From the company's point of view, the rotation has an additional benefit: it develops large numbers of executives who are experienced in many aspects of the business. More than in any other company I have known, Western Electric executives tend to look at problems from a broad company-wide perspective, instead of from the narrower viewpoint of the engineer, the plant manager, or the accountant. Most of their top men have held all those posts. There's never a dearth of qualified management people available for promotion.

When you think of the thousands upon thousands of executives who unwillingly depart the executive suite each month, shouldn't more be done to reduce the damage and costs to the company and the men?

And when you look at the many positive alternatives

to dismissal, you wonder why they're not used more often.

One of those alternatives is simply a policy of no dismissals at all. It seems inconceivable that such a policy (or non-policy) could work. So let's look at a place where it seems to have worked very well indeed.

Hired
for Life

WHAT WOULD HAPPEN TO THE PERFORMANCE OF
YOUR MANAGEMENT GROUP IF THERE WERE NO FIR-
INGS? If, once you were hired, you were guaranteed a job
for life?

Would employees and executives drift into comfortable
lethargy? Would your company lose its ability to compete
aggressively? Without the fear of dismissal, how would
your managers perform?

Don't jump to the conclusion that your company would
slide downhill immediately. For this remarkable state of

Walking the Executive Plank

affairs—a world of no firing and a lifetime job guarantee—
is in effect today in Japan. Yes, Japan, America's toughest
industrial competitor. Your most aggressive, most skilled,
most innovative commercial opponent. Makes you wonder,
doesn't it, about some of our basic management values?
Are they fact or myth? Japan's practice makes you wonder.
Doesn't anyone ever get fired from a management post
in a Japanese company?

"If an executive commits a felony, he will be discharged. But that's about all. There was a case in Tokyo,
not long ago, where a drunken supervisor beat up an employee. He was discharged. But he took it to court, and he
won back his management job. The basis of his victory
was that he was drunk; therefore, he hadn't really known
what he was doing. It wasn't his real nature, and therefore,
it wasn't grounds for dismissal. This sort of case is unusual,
because you rarely ever hear of a management executive
in Japan being fired."

These are the comments of Samuel Ishikawa, an American of Japanese parentage, whose public relations firm,
Masaoka-Ishikawa & Associates in New York, specializes in
foreign trade and governmental affairs problems for Japanese corporations in the United States. Mr. Ishikawa has
spent much of his time and business life in Japan, dealing
with the senior management of Japanese corporations.

One reason, he says, why so few dismissals occur in
Japan is the intense care with which junior executives or
management trainees are selected in the first place. The
best jobs often go to graduates of Tokyo University. The
government seeks them out too. If you were a young Japanese student, you would know that your first job, whether
with the government, a major company or a small company,
will determine your life style from your twenties until the
day you die. Getting into the best university, getting good

grades in the university, therefore becomes tremendously important to a Japanese young man.

"I've seen some of these youngsters cramming to take their college entrance examinations," Mr. Ishikawa says. "It's almost cruel. The results will affect their whole life. If you make Tokyo University, you know that no matter how dumb you are, you'll still be hired by one of the top corporations.

"We have the same thing here in America, but to a much lesser degree. A Harvard degree means something more than a degree from a rural, isolated college in the South. But the difference is greater in Japan. Here you know that even if you attend a small college, you can improve yourself; you can quit your job and change over to something better. But in Japan, the chances are that if you can land a job with only a small company, that's where you're going to be for the rest of your life.

"They give you a very severe examination," says Mr. Ishikawa. "They will check your family history. They will do everything possible to check out your educational record, and to determine whether you are suited for the company mentally, philosophically, and so forth.

"And when they make the decision to hire you, it's certainly the most important decision of your life. There is even a formal ceremony to mark your joining the company. They call you into a room and give you what we'd call a pep talk. You get your ID card as part of the ceremony.

"From the moment you're hired, for the rest of your working life, you're expected to stay with the company. Management devotes a great amount of effort, thought and money to keep you motivated.

"They want you to develop a concern for the success or failure of your company. And usually you do. The system works. Management has all sorts of things to stimulate your incentive. These range from the kind of programs we do here, like company newspapers, to company-owned recreation centers at the beaches or in the mountains where you can go for a vacation. The cost is practically nothing."

Giving a manager security results in a sense of pride about his work. No question about it, according to many knowledgeable observers of the Japanese industrial scene. Japanese managers and workers alike are intensely proud of their work and their companies. They consider that anything bad that happens to their company is a reflection on themselves. If there is something to be proud of, they are proud. If there is something to be ashamed of, they are ashamed for the company and themselves. They take a different attitude toward work than our American managers do. They think nothing of working extra hours. The spirit of joining together and working together toward a common objective dominates the corporate picture.

"One of the first things a sales executive will tell you," Mr. Ishikawa says, "is that his company landed a contract for its products in the U.S.A. or Iran or West Germany, or wherever. I remember one man saying to me, 'You know our electrical equipment is very popular in the U.S.' He said this to me with great pride.

"What a difference from American management people! A typical comment of the type I hear in the U.S. would be, 'You know, we made a half a million dollars on that project.' Our American executives are preoccupied with sales and profits. They are more dollars-and-cents minded. In Japan, you see instead a pride that they've made something that someone else wants enough to buy. They are very proud that they have developed a product in demand abroad, rather than the fact that they have made a million dollars from some deal. Part of this is, of course, a cultural difference. But it does suggest that you can develop highly motivated managers without the fear of dismissal hanging over their head."

"Suppose you were my boss, and I just wasn't performing for you," I said. "What would you do with me if you were managing a company in Japan?"

"I might send you to a branch office," Mr. Ishikawa replied.

"And if I didn't work out there?"

"Then I might have to find a little office for you somewhere, where you could go every day, but you'd have no responsibility whatsoever. Some companies have a special section they might call the Somubu Department, or something like that. We might call it a Liason Office. It consists of a lot of little offices where these men come each morning. They have nothing to do. They'll spend the day reading the paper, sitting around, drinking tea.

"If they had a title before, they keep it. If they were a section chief or a department head previously, that's what they remain," he said. "The only thing is, they have no section or department reporting to them. If they didn't have a title previously, they may be given one now. A title like Consultant or one similar. Of course, the man would have nothing to consult about, and no one to consult with. So he'd drink tea.

"I don't want to give you the impression there are lots of men sitting around in these little offices. There aren't. But there are some. And it is the characteristic Japanese solution to the problem of the incompetent manager. Gets him out of the way where he can do no harm, but doesn't humiliate or embarass him publicly."

I asked Mr. Ishikawa what would happen to my salary if I ended up in the dead-end department.

"Your basic salary would be unchanged," he told me. "However, in the national salary scales, extra monies are given for certain aspects of your job, your degree of responsibility, and so forth. These extra monies would be taken away because your responsibilities would be less."

"Isn't there some way I could get fired from a Japanese management post?"

"Not for incompetence. If you simply weren't able to do the job, you'd receive another assignment. But you would not be discharged. Seniority plays an important part in corporate assignments, and as long as you put in your time, you'll eventually make a top position. That might be a section chief, bureau chief, or department head.

"Suppose I drank too much sake and got drunk and abused the boss. Wouldn't he have to fire me then?"

"He'd probably give you a tongue-lashing, and that would be about it. Or he might tell you to take a couple of weeks off and think things over," Mr. Ishikawa declared.

"In the Japanese culture, is it inconceivable that I might go into the boss and lose my temper?" I inquired.

"Well, you know, even the language is different. If you speak proper Japanese, you'd use a different language to your superior than you would use to your equals. Sort of like the subtle differences between *vous* and *tu* in French, but to a far greater extent.

"Just to illustrate. The language women use is different. There are slight differences. Many American GI's came back from the war speaking female Japanese. You knew immediately where they learned the language. It sounded like young girls talking. There are certain words that only young girls would use, and these were the words the American GI's were using. So in Japanese business organizations, you can detect from listening to the language who is the boss, who are the equals, who are the subordinates. If I were your boss, I'd speak to you slightly differently than if you were my boss. The Japanese language is quite subtle in its expressions, and there would be ways you could tell off the boss without using abusive language."

"Doesn't anybody ever get fired?"

"Yes, I do recall one case. The president of a company, in fact, a friend of mine, got angry with one of his top executives and fired him. He said, 'You go take a rest for a couple of years.' The fellow went off and found a position with one of his relatives who owned a small firm and he became sort of an adviser to him. He received nominal pay, for the sake of appearances, and on top of that, he was receiving severance pay from his former employers.

"At the end of four years, he was brought back to the company and he's one of their top vice-presidents now. That's very unusual. Unusual on two counts. First, in getting fired. Second, in getting rehired by the same company. That's almost the only case I can think of.

"A Japanese company feels it can't discharge anyone because dismissal practically condemns you to permanent hardship. It's almost like saying, 'We're putting you on the unemployment rolls for the rest of your life.'

"Also, you can't conceal a previous job failure by manipulation of your resume. In the U.S.A., you might explain away a period of unemployment by saying that you had been travelling abroad, or in certain fields, that you had been free-lancing. That can't be done in Japan.

"There, your resume is kept quite complete from the day you are born. Your resume will show your education in careful detail, and your employment history from the day you began. If there is a gap, it will show immediately. In a closed society, it's easy to check out someone and find out who he is and what he's been doing. Much easier to do in Kyoto than in Kalamazoo."

"If—once you're hired—you're expected to stay for life, then how does the Japanese economy meet the staffing needs of new and rising companies?" I asked Mr. Ishikawa.

"It becomes a real problem," he told me. "The competent executive hesitates to abandon the company that has treated him well. He thinks not twice but many times before leaving. Suppose the new company fails? Suppose the new technology doesn't work? You may find yourself out on the labor market, and pay a harsh penalty for the entire remaining years of your life.

"For this reason, it becomes especially important for a struggling young enterprise to associate itself with a respected industrial leader, a great entrepreneur, who may be virtually a father figure in the Japanese economy. The participation of such a leader seeks to reassure prospective employees that their risk in job-switching is minimal."

Japan has become such a major factor in world commerce and industry that its internal management policies are closely scrutinized by management leaders in other countries. Why has the Japanese system been so successful? Should it be copied abroad? Or have traditions such as these retarded the growth of the Japanese economy?

I asked Sam Ishikawa for his opinions based on almost 20 years of first-hand observation and comparison.

"Any American who visits a Japanese factory, even the most successful one, will wonder why all those people are working there," he says. "My opinion—not a confirmed fact, but just an informed guess—is that we'd have perhaps 20% fewer people doing the same job in the U.S. There's certainly a less efficient use of labor than in the United States, from factory worker to line and staff managers.

"For instance, I always wonder about the group of people known as the tea haulers. All they do all day long is haul tea around to the other employees. These are loyal employees who receive the same base wage scale as the others. They can gradually move upward from hauling tea to a clerical job.

"Under the Japanese system, when business is bad, people don't get laid off, neither factory workers or managers. They get furloughed. The company keeps them on the payroll at whatever it can afford, say three-quarters pay for doing nothing. That's one reason why Americans are wrong if they think Japan is competing on the basis of low labor costs."

It probably maintains loyalty and close ties with the company. But it also adds to production costs. And perhaps it increases inefficiency. So I inquired of Mr. Ishikawa how Japanese professional managers feel about their system as a whole.

"The problem is being widely discussed in Japanese management organizations," Mr. Ishikawa says. "Typically, you hear comments that management should be able to rid itself of incompetent people. But at the same time, they caution that if management can feel free to fire employees indiscriminately, then managers themselves should be able to change jobs equally freely and no longer need be too loyal to their companies.

"They're weighing the pros and cons. Thus far, most people seem to be coming to the conclusion that the present practice may not be the most efficient way to run industry, but it is probably best suited to the Japanese character.

"Of course, Japan is a country that's undergoing very rapid economic and social change. There is a tremendous generation gap in Japan—much wider and deeper than here. You must remember that Japan lost a tremendous number of men during the war. So you now have a gap between the manager—in his 50's—and the younger executives in their 30's, with nothing in-between. It remains to be seen how the younger generation will feel about the paternalism that is so characteristic of Japanese industry.

"One Japanese industrialist who spends a large amount of time in the United States, and whose business interests here give him broad familiarity with American management practices said to me, 'Five or six years ago, I strongly advocated changes in our ways of doing things. Hiring and firing more freely, and so on. When you hire a young man, don't give him a life-time commitment. When you fire a man, do it without feeling you're bringing him endless humiliation.

"But now I'm no longer so sure. I've noticed that when some of our companies follow this western approach, some of the workers we've trained to a point of being valuable leave to accept other positions. Usually, it's the better men that leave, the ones with more initiative and brains.

"It is really a great loss to the company. Maybe our old system was the best after all."

Clearly, each system, the American and the Japanese, has advantages and disadvantages. But the comparison suggests to this observer, at least, that a middle ground might combine the best features of each system: much greater care in selection, much greater reluctance to fire, taken from the Japanese. Plus the American custom of termination of incompetents, instead of caging them in little rooms with non-existent duties.

Such a new system might realistically combine the best of both Japanese and American practice. It would be more efficient and more humane. And a selfish bonus for my fellow American management consultants: we wouldn't have to face competition from all those "consultants" available in between their tea-drinking and newspaper-reading.

Before
the Axe
Falls

EVERY MANAGEMENT EXPERT PRESENTS AS HIS
FIRST ARTICLE OF CREDO THAT YOU NEVER SHOULD
FIRE AN EXECUTIVE (OR ANYBODY) WITHOUT AD-
VANCE WARNING. It would be indecent to terminate a
man's services without first having given him a chance to
improve as a result of your warning. If he can improve
and keep his job, everybody's ahead: he, you and the company.

This sounds quite obvious but it isn't. In too many
cases I've seen, a warning is not just that, but merely a

routine precursor of dismissal. The man is not expected to improve. Sometimes, improvement isn't even wanted from him. Somebody has decided he must go, and the warning is intended primarily to be recorded in the personnel files, not to influence his behavior.

Over and over again, when I routinely asked top executives how they had warned subordinates before dismissal, I would discover that their so-called warnings amounted to nothing more than vague indications of dissatisfaction.

You can practically guarantee that a warning won't improve a man's performance if you don't want it to. Just tell him his work isn't meeting your standards, or that he hasn't got the right attitude, or that he irritates people. Even if he wanted to improve, how could he possibly know what the "right" attitude is supposed to be, or how he could stop irritating "people"? (That word usually means "the boss.") Such criticism is much too vague to be useful. It's hard enough for us to accept any criticism, much less vague generalities and expressions of evanescent corporate dissatisfaction.

"Unless there's a basic change, I'm going to have to consider letting you go. You had better change your ways." That was the warning Todd Durniak got one month before the curtain fell on his job. He never did figure out where he failed.

Eli Fellows, who was in charge of the computer room in a good-sized mutual fund told me, "My boss called me in and gave me what he called my first, second, and final warning all at once. He said, 'You seem more interested in your programmers and operators than you do in the management of this company. Unless there's a change, we will assume you're not interested in continuing your relationship here.' I assume he meant I wasn't sufficiently deferential to him. He never spelled it out. But two weeks later,

Before the Axe Falls

I was given the pink slip." (Eli didn't mean that literally; giving out dismissal notices printed on pink paper is a custom long since abandoned in industry.)

"To warn a person is meaningless," says William DeMond, an executive personnel expert based in Chicago. "You have to discuss with him specifically where his performance is deficient. You have to tell him what will constitute acceptable performance by your standards. You must spell out to an employee exactly what he has to do and how he can go about improving his results."

Mr. DeMond told me he goes so far as to ask the executive whether the desired improvements are clearly understood. He probes whether personal problems lie hidden behind the job performance problem. Is the executive having personal problems at home? Are there indications of an alcohol problem, or drugs? Mr. DeMond watches sensitively for clues, but at the same time says he tries to avoid overstepping the bounds of business relationships.

Could he give me an example of the kind of warnings he thought ought to be given? Certainly he could. "We had a young fellow in a conglomerate where I was working. He was serving as assistant to the president," Mr. DeMond said. "He was supposed to be seeking out acquisitions and mergers for us.

"First of all, his work was shoddy. He came in with half-baked ideas and proposals that hadn't been thought through or carefully checked for accuracy of detail. That was bad enough, and the president told him so. But on top of that, he wasn't sticking to the job we gave him. If we didn't watch him, he'd go off wandering in other directions. The president finally told him to lay off everything except the search for attractive merger possibilities. Forget everything else.

"He had a number of objectionable personal habits

too," Bill DeMond added. "His office was down the hall from the president's. He had the habit of walking through the executive suite and picking up mail on the secretaries desks. The boss told him to cut that out too.

"And he did. He did change. He stopped reading other people's mail, and he began putting more careful work into his merger possibility reports. That improvement lasted for a short period of time, and then he started sliding off again. Eventually we had to let him go. You might say he quit by invitation."

Sheldon Jaffe, a New York advertising agency man, told me how he summoned the agency's business development executive, the man assigned to cultivate potential clients. "I told him quite bluntly he was failing on three counts. One: his job was to bring in new business, and he wasn't bringing it in. Two: his expenses were running much higher than they should. Three, his expense account was filled with fraud."

Was that a warning or a firing? "It was a warning. I was telling him to bring in some accounts." Did it work? "No." Did he bring in business? "No. I couldn't even get him to listen. I discussed each of these points with him a number of times, and there was just no progress. All he would say to me was, 'You just don't understand. You have no feel for the situation. These things take time.' "

Jaffe told me about another case, the ad agency's production manager. There were indications of poor management in the department, Jaffe said, so he called in the manager for a discussion. "I talked about the specific problems," he said, "but without talking about his lack of overall performance. Just the specific problems. As our talk went on, he assured me he was working very hard. I believed that. He really was trying. And I was impressed by that because, you know, I'm a pretty hard worker myself.

I have a tendency to judge productivity in terms of the number of hours you put in, and measurements of whatever it is you are doing, how many letters you send or phone calls you handle, or meetings you attend.

"But there is a big difference between working hard and working smart. The real question should be, what did you accomplish? In terms of the production manager, I found he had lots of meeting with printers, engravers and suppliers, but the meetings didn't result in improved service or reduced costs nor did they help to move the agency ahead in any way. I let him go.

"Then I had another man in our media department. He was a poor money manager. We paid salaries twice a month, but this fellow was always running short before payday and having to borrow advances of $50 or $100. I discussed his problem with him. I was positive and specific but I also was firm. He assured me he'd get firm control of his spending habits. I gave him 30 days, but I didn't tell him that. I just made a note in my Day-Timer to take another look in a month.

"There had been no change. I would say this man was a hopeless case. I couldn't live with him any longer. And I didn't like the idea of a man who was financially irresponsible getting involved in recommendations on how to spend our clients money. So after 30 days, I called him and said, 'You're going to have to leave us. There's been no improvement.' "

A company president (who won't let me use his name) told me how his attempted warning had failed:

"I failed to get Hubert Urrows to change his ways. His work habits were too firmly set. You see, our company had come through a period of plenty. We had good profits in spite of ourselves. In those days, Hubie hadn't had to work hard to look good. Well, now times had become rough

48

Walking the Executive Plank

for us. I think it's awfully difficult for an executive to roll up his sleeves and go to work again after years in an easier pattern. Hubie had acquired the self-image of a manager who discusses problems, delegates work to others, and has two-hour lunches. He figured he had worked harder than anyone else in his earlier days, so why should he have to work hard again? It just wasn't realistic for me to expect him to change. He didn't." It was one more case where a warning did not prove effective in preventing dismissal.

Despite this long series of unproductive discussions, my friend, Alvin Vogel, president of the highly successful Securance Corporation of New York, remains firmly convinced that warning can often improve an unsatisfactory performance. "The responsibility of management is to improve efficiency. If a manager can't improve the performance of a man under him, there's no reason for him to have his job." Al insists the key to success lies in how you give your warning.

"You don't improve a manager's performance by threatening him with dismissal, even by implication. If a man thinks he must improve or lose his job, then he's already lost to the company. I don't care whether you call it firing or termination or 'requesting your resignation' or whatever Madison Avenue fandango you want to use. Once you convey that idea, the man's usefulness to you is gone forever. He'll start looking for another job, simply because he knows he's not satisfying you with his results.

"This is more than a matter of words," Al told me. "It's central to my position that you help people perform, not by threats but by taking a positive approach. You know the old saying, 'A glass of water is either half full or half empty.' I prefer to take the positive approach. I don't say to a man, 'You're not doing your job well.' I say, 'Let's take a look at the figures and see what you really have to do to earn a living. Let's see how you can improve production.' Sometimes it works."

However, I asked a whole group of my friends in corporate management if they could recall single case of a man who improved his performance and saved his job as a result of a warning. My friends usual answer was, "If you let me think about it for a while, I'm sure I'll remember a case like that." They never did. In fact, in my experience, involving close management relationships over long periods of time, I don't think I've ever seen anyone change significantly. Experience suggests that even the best managers can improve performance only within a very narrow framework. For example, if a manager is performing only 25% of the job, maybe a good boss could help him improve to 30% or 35%, but not much more than that.

Then why all the corporate insistence on warning before firing? Why is it so important to the corporate personnel director and the president alike?

I think the reason is that the act of warning absolves us from guilt when we subsequently perform the surgical rite of dismissal. That's a valid reason.

The head of the design engineering department in a Philadelphia electronics firm summarized his philosophy this way: "I personally have great faith in human beings. Maybe it is because I am a Quaker. I believe every person is capable of constantly improving himself.

"When I have to warn an employee," he told me, "I always level with him, but I think it rarely has any effect. After all, it is up to each person to decide if he wants to improve himself, and many people may not choose to."

Others may be unable to. "It's impossible to change people," a Dayton, Ohio bank officer told me. "You may persuade a man to make some little surface changes, but you're not going to change his personality or his psychology."

A man is no fool. If you call in an executive and start criticizing his work, even if he doesn't get the message the first time, he'll get it the second. His job is in danger. So why do all these managers agree that they can't remember any man improving after warnings?

I believe that by asking the unsatisfactory executive to change his ways, they were asking him to do something of which he was incapable. In asking him to change his standard of values, or to remove irritants which reflected his inner feelings, they were asking him to become something that he wasn't and couldn't be. It's no surprise that it didn't happen and isn't likely to happen.

I recall an acquaintance of mine who had been fired from a production post in a shoe equipment manufacturing firm after repeated warnings of unsatisfactory performance. I recently asked him whether he had realized exactly what was expected of him and where he was failing. He replied, "I knew what they wanted. I tried to give it to them. But my style of supervision wasn't what they wanted. I tried to adapt, but I couldn't. I lost my own metabolism, my own fingerprints. Whatever I did came out like me, not like the boss wanted. I simply couldn't be a carbon copy of him. I tried. I stayed with it. But it just didn't work."

What he was saying, of course, was that to change his style of supervision would have required a change in his personality. He didn't feel he could do this, and, indeed, he wasn't able to do it.

A retail executive in Montgomery, Alabama, recalled similar reactions to a job warning. "I couldn't have changed even if I had wanted to. First of all, I didn't like my boss at that time. I was hostile towards him. I thought then he was stupid, and I still think so today. I think I'm a fairly good actor, but I simply couldn't have concealed my attitude from him completely. I didn't change. The boss didn't change. So he fired me."

Some executives may be convinced *they* don't need to change; *you* do. "When you criticize a man," Arthur Mehan, Foundation executive, says, "his tendency is to go home and discuss it with his wife. She'll usually take the view that you don't appreciate him any more. His friends at the company are certainly going to take his side also, because 'management' is always the enemy—even if he and they themselves are part of management. It's very hard to be objective and say, 'O.K., now what am *I* doing wrong?' He'd rather blame the boss than change his ways."

Are you therefore wrong in warning your poor performers? Is it a futile gesture? I think not. Warnings are probably like the doctor's placebo pills: they don't cure anything, but they often make you feel better just for having taken them.

7
The Technique of Corporate Surgery

TO TELL THE TRUTH OR NOT? That's the biggest single dilemma you face when you decide to fire someone. At least I think so, judging from my own experiences.

It's not a simple question of truth-or-lies, black-or-white, yes-or-no, all-or-nothing. It's a question of degree, of shadings, of nuances, of the precise words you use when you terminate a man. And beneath all this, there is fundamentally a question of ethics and morality you'll have to decide for yourself.

Take a man like Ralph de Sherbinin. You've decided to

fire him. You have an open-and-shut case that while he has been functioning as head of your Accounts Receivable department, he has done a poor job. There are measurements of such things, and by any reasonable standard of measurement, he's failed. In this not-so-hypothetical case, Ralph hasn't brought in the money from delinquent accounts in the proper amounts and at the proper times. His performance could be judged both by comparison with his predecessor's, and with the current history of other companies in the same field, who exchange credit data among themselves. You could judge his failure by excessive personnel turnover in his department, and by excessive absenteeism. You pick a measurement; the likelihood is, Ralph has failed by any standard. So you decide to terminate his services. Ralph hasn't worked for you so very long that he has any right to feel securely locked into his job. He's had warnings previously. Now the time has come to act.

In Ralph's case, this doesn't happen to be an easy thing to do. You like the man personally. He's honest. He's decent. He's certainly tried his best. (Unfortunately, no job is currently open into which he would fit, so a transfer is out of the question). What will you tell him is the reason for his dismissal?

You could tell him the truth. Most managers, most personnel men and most corporate psychologists advocate this. In the long run, they say, everyone is better off by telling Ralph the truth. If you accept this technique, called F-1 and held almost unanimously by the experts, you might say, "Ralph, I'm sorry but I'm going to have to let you go. Your work has not been satisfactory. You're entitled to know the reasons. For one thing, Ralph your collections have not been satisfactory. The percentage of past-due receivables has been climbing since you took over. As a matter of fact, we checked, and it's higher in your department than it is among our competitors. We asked them their figures, and there's no doubt about your poor performance.

"Then another thing, Ralph. The way you've handled the people in your department hasn't been satisfactory to us. We've noticed that a lot of people under your supervision have been quitting the company, even despite that last pay raise we gave them. And we see the time sheets, and there's much more absenteeism and lateness than there should be. This is your responsibility as the head of the department.

"So, I'm sorry, Ralph, but we've had to decide that this has been an unsatisfactory performance, and we're letting you go."

Now before we get into a discussion of this particular way of announcing the reasons for dismissal, let me give you an alternative method, F-2, so that you can consider the choice.

"Ralph, I have some disappointing news for you. You've been in this job for almost a year now, and you've certainly been working hard at it. We know you've tried. But it just hasn't been working out the way we hoped. Haven't you felt that?

"So, we're going to have to call it quits as of Friday afternoon. You've been very conscientious, and we know you've done your best, but it hasn't been right. Things haven't gone right in the department, and we think this is the best thing to do."

At which point, Ralph is certainly going to say, "What do you mean, it hasn't been right? Can't you tell me specifically? Did I do something wrong? What is it?"

According to Technique F-2 you then are supposed to say, "No, Ralph, you haven't done anything wrong. It's just that things haven't worked out as we hoped they would. It has been a good try, but we think it's better this way. So you're going to get two months separation pay, plus your vacation pay. That's another three weeks. I have the check right here for you."

You can be sure that friend Ralph will then protest, "But I'm entitled to know why you're doing this to me."

And here, the script for Technique F-2 calls for you to say, "No, Ralph, I don't think we'd accomplish anything by getting into all the details. That wouldn't solve anything. The main thing is, you tried. We tried, and it just didn't work out. I think that's enough."

Technique F-1 tells Ralph exactly why he's being dropped from the corporate payroll, and Technique F-2 gives him some vague doubletalk. That sums up the difference.

I personally admit to being troubled by this choice every time a decision is my hands. I suppose I resolve it somewhere between the two extremes. Maybe it tells you something about my personality when I mention that my natural inclination would be to use Technique F-2. I can't recommend it to you in the face of the near-unanimous preference of both psychologists and personnel men for Technique F-1, but you ought to consider the arguments on both sides.

The main points in favor of telling an executive exactly why you're dismissing him are these:

First of all, he's entitled to know, as a matter of plain decency. Even though he may not accept the correctness of your reasons, he will be less inclined to believe that your decision is arbitrary or based on personal pique.

Second, he may benefit from your criticism. When he knows exactly where his performance has been considered unsatisfactory, he may make a special effort to improve in these areas. This would be impossible for him to do if he isn't told his specific shortcomings.

Third, the company may benefit from getting its position on the record. Management may less often be accused of improper dismissals, or charges of discrimination, if they've told the victim exactly why he's being dismissed.

"The way I look at it, firing a manager from a job he's held for a long time is the most traumatic thing a man can experience, short of a divorce." That's the way Win A. Jones, head of a steel warehousing operation, sees it. "People who are fired have a tendency to walk out into the street and say, 'The blankety-blank. He didn't even tell me why.' Even when my supervisors have told him exactly. He just doesn't want to hear it.

"I make it a rule in this company that our supervisors are required to write out the reasons, read them to the man, discuss them with him, and then task him to sign the paper stating that he's heard the contents. Pretty stuffy, don't you think? We'll even give him a copy if he wants it. His signature doesn't mean he agrees with our judgment. It only means he has heard our reasons as we have given them. I tell our supervisors to let the man know why we are not satisfied with him. The franker the better.

"Of course, he doesn't want to hear it. We'll say, 'Jack, you're not performing. Do you understand?' If he parrots back at us, 'You say that I'm not performing,' then we'll tell him again, because it is obvious he's not really hearing us."

In situations like this, it's always a temptation to fall back on excuses. You can tell a man he's being "let go" (Gentlemen don't use the word "firing." It's rude and crude.) because of a cutback, or because of corporate reorganization. And admittedly, says Win A. Jones, it's a temptation. It's easier that way. But he insists, it's a mistake in the long run.

Unless you give a man the honest reasons, there is also the danger that his firing may cause distressing and unwanted anxieties among other employees who don't know the real reasons. In one of the regional trucking companies, an executive told me he had been taken to lunch by his boss one day and told that the company was firing his brother, who worked for the company in another city. The reasons were spelled out, and the executive interpreted the luncheon notification as a thoughtful courtesy. "I guess they didn't want me to get upset," he said. "When I talked to my brother later, he was angry. He felt he had been a victim of circumstances. I asked him if he had really been giving the job all he had, and he admitted he hadn't. After hearing both my boss and my brother, I could hardly be angry at the company."

Now don't conclude that the weight of evidence favors F-1. Consider the case for Technique F-2. Humane consideration for the victim, rather than cowardice, say its advocates, motivates the "vague generality" school. A man's most basic instinct, they say, is his instinct for survival. Threaten his opinion of himself, and you create an emotional crisis for him. A man wants to believe he's competent and acceptable to his colleagues. Tell him he's not, and you threaten his whole personality.

So, they say, why specify all the exact areas where the executive has failed? What do you accomplish except to give him pain? He can't accept the validity of your criticism without accepting his own inadequacy. And no one will accept that. As Charles Salamanca, a friend of mine in a medical equipment and supply company, says, "They usually come away from the situation saying that something is wrong with the company or the boss."

Owen Michaels has a firing style close to F-2. He says, "I try to fire in a calm way and to depersonalize it. I'll say, 'We have agreed that the job requires thus-and-so and you have tried and it hasn't worked out. It is therefore in the best interest of the company that you no longer be asso-

Walking the Executive Plank

ciated with us. Probably it's in your best interests too, because there is no future for you here. There will be no raises for you here, and you will just become frustrated and get an ulcer. Perhaps you will fit in better in some other environment.' "

If you try to spell out all the details, something else happens, say the few solitary souls in the F-2 camp. Sylvan Snyder, a friend of mine in Rockford, Illinois, went through this and told me, "Sometimes the guy wants you to discuss every individual instance where you say he failed. You do that, and you'll find yourself getting involved in an endless discussion over the details. Did this happen? Who said what to whom? You can't win that one, and neither can he. It gets messy." Sylvan thinks there's a difference between being frank (which he advocates) and being specific (which he doesn't).

"If you make it personal, 'You did this and you did that,' you defeat the purpose," he says. "There is no sense in destroying a person when you fire him. The company does not benefit in any way. Unless you are a sadist, you don't benefit in any way. So why not part on a low-key, with the approach that he is just not right for the company in that job at this time? We come together not to love each other but to do a particular piece of work. We made a mistake so let's part."

If you happened to read my book, *Survival in the Executive Jungle*, you may remember that I leaned toward Technique F-2 in those days, and I haven't completely abandoned my previous position.

I know many executives who have been fired, some of them quite deservedly. Not one, as far as I can tell, has profited from the experience of being told the details of his alleged failures. Not one, insofar as I can see, has said to himself afterwards, "Maybe the boss was right when he criticized me for such-and-such. I'd better work harder to do a better job next time." Instead, the dismissed executives have gone right on to their next jobs with the same shortcomings and the same problems arising. Psychologically, it's much easier that way than to admit that maybe you've failed.

Grant Sbrocco, an experienced personnel man in a forest products company out in Oregon, sums up the case for F-2 this way: "It's bad enough to turn the man out of the corporate cabin and into the woods by himself. Why axe his pride on top of it? He'll need it to survive."

You decide for yourself.

8

Double Standards

YOU CAN'T BE A MANAGER IN A BIG CORPORATION
THESE DAYS WITHOUT BEING INTENSELY AWARE OF
RACE AND SEX AS FACTORS IN HIRING AND PROMO-
TIONS. Pressures to hire and promote blacks and women.
Charges of discrimination made to and by government
agencies. Fear of loss of corporate good will. Quotas. Af-
firmative action programs. Equal opportunity programs.
The whole subject is emotionally charged, especially re-
garding black Americans.

Double Standards

Of course there are good reasons why this is so. Since the earliest days of corporate America until recent years, virtually no corporation has been willing to consider blacks for management posts.

The racially discriminatory pattern doesn't always begin at the corporate hiring office; sometimes, it rarely even exists there at all. Blacks got the message in past years that they weren't wanted in corporations; those few who were qualified spared themselves the pain of rejection by not applying. Others spared themselves the waste of training and academic preparation for jobs that would be closed to them. Their school guidance counselors "protected" them from indignity by channeling them away from college and into service jobs. If they were able to gain admittance to a black college, their college administrator in turn realistically channeled their energies into those few career paths then open, usually in social service, teaching, the ministry, or the law.

All this resulted in predictable consequences. The aerospace company that professed its dedication as an "equal opportunity" employer didn't have its good faith put to the test, because there were few qualified black aerospace engineers to be found at the time.

Today, corporate hiring policies have changed greatly. Some companies now aggressively recruit black executives. But then, in the interests of "fairness," the minute they've been hired, management treats them "like everybody else" and stands by while they fail in disproportionately high numbers. No wonder. If you came from a family where no one before you had ever attended college, a family in which no one had ever before worked for a corporation; if you know hardly anyone who's ever been employed by a major corporation; if you attended a black college whose graduates had rarely been sought for company employment, is it any surprise that you would find yourself in a frightening environment?

No, it isn't "equal opportunity" to put a black man into a corporate job and let him stand or fall "like anyone else." The black manager needs special help and understanding and he should receive it.

As I see it, white managers should make special allowances in hiring black men and women who may seem to lack qualifications or experience. They may never have had a chance to gain that experience. White managers have a responsibility to provide extra training. We have a responsibility to be a bit more patient during a man's learning experience. We have a responsibility to help a black man or woman "make it" in his or her new job.

But once he's receives this compensation for past denial of opportunities, then it's up to the man himself to perform satisfactorily. It's up to him to meet the same standards that other employees or other managers must meet. In any job where human relationships are important, it's his responsibility to make reasonable efforts to get along with his corporate colleagues.

At that point, if he fails—judged by the same standards as you'd judge anyone else—he ought to be fired. To keep an unsatisfactory performer is, in my view, indecent because it implies you should expect less from black managers. That's racism, any way you slice it.

Some companies have had problems with black men who succeeded. They soon wanted promotions to management ranks, exactly as did their white colleagues. The successful blacks refused to be grateful to the company that employed them originally, believing that they were receiving only rights that black people should have received a century ago.

In some companies, black professionals who have failed, and who should be dismissed, have become a problem too. Management simply doesn't want to fire them. Partly, it fears having to defend itself against racial discrimination charges before government agencies or a court of law. But another part of the problem is sometimes a company's honest intention to end discrimination within its ranks, and a feeling that it should accept lower performance by black employees. Some companies are determined to make Equal Opportunity work, and avoidance of firing blacks is part of their commitment.

From a management viewpoint, I believe it's absolutely wrong to set lower standards for black employees, just as wrong as it is to set higher requirements for blacks before they can win promotion.

Black people demand, and rightly, that they be treated on the basis of their ability, not their skin color. They object to the concept that a double standard should apply; that they need to be twice as qualified as a white man to receive a promotion, or only half as qualified to keep their jobs.

"Utopia for blacks is that distant land where every person will be appraised on his own merit," writes Dr. Stuart A. Taylor, associate professor at the Graduate School of Business of Harvard University, himself black.

Consider the damaging effects on the rest of your organization if you keep an unsatisfactory black employee on your staff. The others rightly reason that if you allow him to get away with something, they're entitled to also. Instead of building the mutuality of respect that's essential to good human relations and effective management, you encourage contempt and racial discord.

When you set a double standard based on color, you

Walking the Executive Plank

create a whole bag of problems that ought to be avoided. I'll cite some examples from my personal experience. Take this case, which happened in 1969 near Jacksonville, Florida. Ron Braithwaite, a supervisor in a materials testing laboratory, was the only black professional in his entire company. He had responsibility for testing samples of a finished product, randomly selected as they came off the assembly line. His staff had to make certain prescribed measurements, and to record the results.

Braithwaite's boss told me what happened. Braithwaite's staff, he said, often failed to keep records or to complete the necessary sequence of tests on particular product samples. This made the tests on particular product samples useless, and finally Braithwaite got fired.

At this point, the company attorneys feared he might file a discrimination complaint, so they joined the investigation being conducted by the personnel department. The company lawyers noticed that only a few months before, Braithwaite had been given a salary increase. They properly asked how a salary increase could be squared with charges that his work hadn't been acceptable.

The personnel department came up with the honest answer. The increase, they said, was a cost-of-living increase and had nothing to do with the quality of his performance. Their records had been carefully kept; they substantiated the company's position, and when the firing went to arbitration, the company was upheld.

But that isn't the point of the story. The point is that Ron Braithwaite's boss should have fired him five years ago. According to his boss, Braithwaite hadn't been doing his job satisfactorily even then, but he was kept on because he was the only black in a supervisory position. So his job was done badly for five years. That was no service to Braithwaite, to the company, or to the customers.

Take the case of the supervisor of the Mail Room in a Randolph Street office. He was black, as his predecessors had been, for supervisor of the Mail Room is known as a "black job" in many companies. This fellow had a mad-on as far as the world was concerned. The office manager, a "liberal," tolerated his surliness for a long time. People in the office agreed that the supervisor couldn't seem to talk to anyone decently. His unpleasantness created a mood of irritability and annoyance throughout the premises. If he had been white, he would have been fired a long time ago. But mistaken goodwill kept him on, because management had set up double standards based on color.

A few years ago, when it became popular in certain corporate circles to have a "house black" on premises, one jewelry company went out and found itself a personable, bright and pleasant school teacher named Matt Howell. He was hired as the first Negro salesman the company ever had. To show its good intent, the company assigned the new man to call upon some of its most prestigious accounts in New York City. The salesman's draw was reasonable if not good; certainly better money than he had been earning as a teacher.

But Matt Howell didn't make it. He knew nothing about the jewelry business or about selling, and he was trying to learn both at the same time he was out on the firing line. He found he couldn't relate to his customers; the store buyers spoke a language of their own, and they came from a different background than his. The poor man nearly went out of his mind. He couldn't sleep nights for worry of failure. He was miserable. Soon he started drinking, and he started coming late.

This was a warning flag of trouble, so pretty soon the sales manager went to the vice-president and asked permission to fire Matt. "You can't fire him," said the personnel boss. "I won't give you an o.k. to do it. You didn't hire him because he was a good salesman or because he had the qualities the job required. You hired him because he was black. And until the time that he becomes white, you have no basis for firing him. So you better go back and find a place where he can serve you usefully."

The status of women in corporations parellels that of black executives. In many industries, no management opportunities exist for women, so women logically will not train for jobs not open to them. Therefore, few if any trained women are available. This makes it convenient for some managements to justify their policies of having no women in management, even at junior levels. Personnel policies continue under the direction of males who simply can't visualize women in posts of authority and responsibility.

It's an unbreakable chain. Or was, until recently when Women's Lib consciousness burst explosively on the nation. Now women are beginning to attend management training courses and graduate schools of business in significant numbers. Every once in a while now, I come across a woman in a junior management post in some company where there were none before.

But, man, has she got problems with the male executives! Instead of training her adequately and then expecting her to perform like anyone else, neither better or worse, she becomes a sex symbol for 33% of the executives. (This includes those who are repelled by her sexually as well as those whom she attracts.) She becomes a Mother Symbol for another 26.57% of the executives, who transfer to her all the attitudes they previously held toward their own mothers (13.28% love, 13.29% hate). She becomes a Daughter Symbol for 36.82% of the male executives. (35.91% want to father her protectively; 0.91% would accept her if only she were a son). The remaining 3.61%

either like the idea of equal rights for women or would accept anyone in preference to the unpleasant guy who occupied the same job previously.

What should be your corporate policy toward hiring and firing of minority managers and executives? The answer is equal opportunity. Equal opportunity to succeed. Equal opportunity to fail. Equal opportunity to get fired.

9

Walking the Corporate Plank

"GET 'EM OUT QUICK."

That's the overwhelming recommendation, in fact, the almost unanimous opinion of top management on timing an executive dismissal. In the judgment of many corporate executives, there isn't any room for discussion.

Two weeks notice? No. Everyone agrees it's a mistake. The company will be better off if you give the discharged executive two weeks additional pay "in lieu of notice" and ask him to leave immediately. The higher the rank of the corporate executive, the quicker he should be turned out to pasture, once he's been notified of your decision. One company president expresses the opinion that when a man is fired or resigns voluntarily, he should leave "that minute." This is more than an abstract phrase with him. Just recently, his executive vice president came to him and unexpectedly said, "I've decided to leave the company in about six months. I want to make a basic change in the direction of my business life." This announcement gave the president an opportunity to practice what he preached. He seized the opportunity.

"No," he answered firmly, "you're leaving right now. I can't have an executive vice-president on my hands who is not spending his full time thinking about the company. I'd appreciate it if you'd leave today." The president believes that once a person has decided to leave, his interim presence is highly disruptive to the organization. "It's like surgery," he told me. "It's best done and over with."

A senior vice-president in a national bank, a man who does a lot of firing and who seems to enjoy doing it even more than I enjoy eating pizza (which is saying a good deal), told me, "We want them to leave as rapidly as they can. But we ask them courteously to get out. Why burn your bridges behind you? In most cases, the men and women I fire are likely to remain in the banking field. My bank may even be dealing with them at one time or another. So we try to have a gentlemanly parting, rather than an abrupt parting. However, I still ask them to leave immediately." Incidently, I can't help wondering what this vice-president would consider as an "abrupt" parting if he regards immediate departure as "a gentlemanly parting." Maybe "abrupt" means a vigorous shove out the executive door.

But what if the executive does not respond to his ouster in a gentlemanly way? He would hardly be human if he didn't become angry at you and the company for dismissing him. Who knows how and where he may wish to strike back in anger?

If he's been employed in a critical spot like data processing, he's in a position to do severe damage with nothing more than the press of the wrong button on your computer, a button that might instantly wipe clean a reel of tape storing valuable corporate records. Companies are not unsophisticated in these matters, so when a computer man is slated for termination, alarm bells start ringing, figuratively anyway, in the personnel and security departments.

"I remember," comptroller Mansfield Carter told me, "when I fired one of our computer managers because he was doing a lousy job. He thereupon threatened to file a complaint against us with the National Labor Relations Board. He told us he had been planning to organize the computer operators and punch-card people and that we had found out about it, and that's why we were firing him. (Incidentally, that was the first we had heard of it.) He threatened to take all "his" people with him because they were personally loyal to him. He said he was going to screw up the computer programs, which he could have done.

"There were all kinds of threats. His voice went high-pitched and tense. There was much yelling and shouting from me too. I told him he'd have to leave the premises right away. I told him I thought he was a fool; that we had tried to get a job done, and that he had botched things up, and that we had kept him on far longer than he probably deserved."

"Mr. Carter," I interjected, "I'm astonished that you would have had to raise your voice. All these years I've known you, I've regarded you as an exceptionally calm personality. I've never known you to get upset like this."

"Chet," Mansfield Carter replied, "I think 50% he

riled me, and 50% I was trying to show him that this was not the game to play; that I could play the game too. He was threatening me with all sorts of dire consequences if I didn't keep him. This wasn't rational, because the mere fact that he threatened us meant that he could no longer remain. You can't keep people in positions of trust when they respond that way.

"I didn't want the company threatened, and I didn't want him to attempt to carry out any of his threats, so I said, 'We can be just as tough as you are.' I had him escorted out to the parking lot immediately. The only thing missing from the scene was the playing of the Rogue's March and that roll of the drums they use in the Marine Corps when they catch a thief in the ranks. It was all over in 20 minutes."

Some companies have developed more sophisticated ways to accomplish immediate physical ouster. Once they notify an executive he's terminated, they want him removed from his normal working area to avoid demoralizing his former colleagues. If a manager takes the bad news "like a gentleman," they may be willing to provide him with a base of operations during his employment hunt, and especially, a place to make phone calls and receive messages.

A national products manufacturer, for instance, maintains a small suite of offices in New York's Pan Am Building* for about-to-be-dismissed executives. When the company decides to terminate your services, they transfer you to one of these offices in the Pan Am Building. You are told nothing about a termination. You retain your title, and your secretary goes with you. But when you arrive, you discover that you have no duties to perform. Your inter-office mail has already been cut off by orders to the mail

*If you don't live in New York and therefore don't know the building. I should specify that the company isn't Pan American World Airways.

room. And it begins to dawn on you that the time has come to prepare for your departure from the corporation.

Actually, that's the way it was in the early days. Today, everyone knows that the "Pan Am Suite" is this corporation's Devil's Island. There's no Papillon-like escape back to the company headquarters through Manhattan's shark-infested waters. When your transfer to "Pan Am" comes through, you know you're through too.

The company will be gentle and kindly about letting you stay and use the telephone in your job hunt. Your secretary can divide her time between solving the daily crossword puzzle and answering your phone calls. The company has WATS telephone lines, so it costs them practically nothing for the few long distance telephone calls you may make in pursuit of your next job. Average duration in the Pan Am offices is about four months, but one man stayed over a year before finally departing. Meanwhile, you receive your accumulated vacation pay plus severance pay based on length of service. When your pay stops, your secretary is called back to headquarters, but you're allowed to stay on as long as you wish.

This civilized method costs the company little except for the office rental. And it serves the purpose of removing the executive from the scene immediately. With the "Pan Am Routine," the boss doesn't even have to wait until Friday morning just before lunch to give you your dismissal news. He can do it anytime at all.

A less civilized method was used by corporate heads who executed their dismissals not in person, not by memo, not even by telephone calls to the victim, but by a telephone answering service.

Yes, it really happened.

One Monday morning, top management circulated a formal (and completely unexpected) announcement that corporate headquarters would be moved to Texas. As soon as detailed plans were completed, the announcement said, top management would advise the department heads who in turn would be expected immediately to notify their staffs.

On Friday of the same week came the second announcement, also in a formal mimeographed memo: decisions were now being made as to who would be invited to move to Texas with the company and who would be left behind to terminate their operations. Formal and personal announcements would be distributed to the executives on the following Monday morning. But you could find out immediately where you stood by phoning a special telephone number, beginning Saturday morning.

Did top management really think anyone would wait until Monday when his job was hanging uncertainly in the air? Of course not. So everyone phoned the telephone number on Saturday morning. And an unfamiliar voice, the voice of a private answering service operator, took the call. "Would you give me your name and the number on your I.D. card identification?" she'd ask pleasantly. You'd respond, and hold your breath.

"Oh, I'm sorry, you're on List #2," she'd say. "That means you won't be going to Texas. The personnel department will be in touch with you by mail, but you won't have to go into your office on Monday. They'll make arrangements to deliver all your personal effects, and so on. I'm sorry. Thank you for calling. Goodbye."

Fired—without reasons and without even knowing who told you. It really happened, exactly as I've described it. And the executives were already off the premises!

Most firings still take place in the office on Friday mornings. A young and still un-toughened manager explains why: "It's easier on me. The fellow cleans out his desk while everyone else is out to lunch, and by the time they get back, he's gone. I don't have to push him out; he pushes himself out because he wants to spare himself the humiliation of facing his peers. If for any reason he needs to come back, he has the week-end to compose himself before he walks in on Monday morning. And the staff has a chance over the weekend to get over the shock."

There's another type of executive, catalogued as Type 236(b) in Burger's Catalog of Executive Types. (Sorry, I can't quote further; this catalog is classified Top Secret.) This man will never make a fuss when you give him the word. Type 236(b) is the perfect gentleman. He won't try to steal your company secrets, if any, or even slip a box of your company's paper clips in his attache case. He will leave promptly, courteously, and with a pleasant smile on his face. He'll never raise questions.

He's already anticipated you. He's a member of the type called counterfeit executives, the men who get fired and fired and fired. When you fire one of these dillies, he thanks you, goes back to his office, makes a few phone calls to your competitors, and by the next Monday morning he may be working again, this time against you.

Firing has come as no surprise to him. He not only expected it to come sooner or later, but he began looking for his next employer the day he came to work for you. A few months after you hired him, when his future still looked bright and rosy, he was already telling the personnel people in other companies that while he was perfectly happy to be working for you, some strains were already beginning to show in your relationship; you "perhaps were a bit jealous of his success." After dropping the hint, he left it there. No elaboration. No specifics. No expressions of discontent. But a year and a half later, after you had weighed his performance and found it wanting, he could plausibly call your competitor's personnel man and remind him of the original conversation. The man I know who did this most successfully held five jobs in different corporations within eleven years. Each job was a higher one, but each company was lower on the scale of American business, as *Forbes* magazine would perhaps rate such matters.

The hiring company, of course, in these cases feels it is acquiring a real plum, a gold-plated plum, a man whom you don't appreciate and whose talents you don't know how to utilize. Since he tells them frankly in each case that you have fired him, they are not inclined to check with you further. Hasn't he anticipated that possibility by saying you personally are competitive with him, and jealous of his success? They put him on their payroll so fast that he doesn't need to be encouraged to leave your premises.

Higher and higher in the corporate hierarchy moves your Departed One, but for shorter and shorter durations in each post. Toward the end of his meteoric rise, his duration in any post can usually be estimated at about 18 months. And when there are no more places to go, when his true reputation is all too widely spread in his industry, when he has walked the corporate plank for the last time, the counterfeit executive remains thoroughly and calmly prepared for the next step. He has his own memo, already mimeographed and ready for release.

It announces the formation of his own management consultant firm.

10
How the
Consultants
See It

THERE IS NOTHING LIKE THE APPEARANCE OF MAN-
AGEMENT CONSULTANTS ON THE CORPORATE SCENE
TO SPREAD THE FEAR OF FIRING IN A COMPANY. It's
a part of corporate folklore that "Management Studies + 30
days = Dismissals." After all, goes the reasoning, hasn't
management brought in consultants to cut costs? The only
fellow who never worries about the consultant's recommendations is the top executive who hired the consultants
in the first place. He feels, usually accurately, that con-

sultants, like anyone else, are hardly likely to bite the hand that etc. So says the gossip at the office water-cooler.

Well, folklore usually contains at least a germ of truth. The connection between consultants and dismissals exists in corporate folklore because the connection exists in reality.

Sometimes, the boss wants to fire a key person, a major executive. But he needs an excuse. The real reason may be that he finds himself irritated by the victim's personality. Or the top boss and the vice-president have been social friends for a dozen years, and it's just too damned awkward to call Harry in and say, "Sorry, fella." Much easier to have a management consultant produce a confidential report saying that Harry's area of responsibility must be eliminated in the new corporate reorganization.

I know one company president who wanted to use his management consultant exactly that way. But he was too subtle about it. He asked the consultants to study the allocation of responsibilities among the various vice-presidents and tell him whether they thought Harry's job was necessary. They apparently didn't get the point. In 30 days, back came their report saying, yes, Harry's job was essential and Harry was doing it very well.

The fools, thought the president. "They're not understanding me. Look," he told them." "I want Harry out. Now you get back in there and find all the reasons why he's got to go." And they did. The report found four major reasons why his job "unfortunately" had to be eliminated.

The management consultants, incidentally, saw nothing unethical about this, and nothing unprofessional about their performance. The partner in charge of this assignment told me, "We're working for the president. He doesn't want this man around. He needs to get Harry out, and we've been hired to help meet his needs."

Walking the Executive Plank

Sometimes management consultants are used to do more than provide excuses for a dismissal already decided upon. Sometimes consultants are asked personally to swing the axe. More than once in my own work, a company head has asked me to formally notify an executive that he's through. Sometimes, he asked me out of his desire to avoid an unpleasant scene. Once I willingly took the job in the mistaken belief that it was the right thing for me to do.

It was in a publishing company. Vice-president Jack Fondilla asked me to do the job. He was an angry man to begin with. He was even angrier at John McLeod, the department head he had decided to fire. Fondilla knew that when the moment of truth came and he had to swing the axe, McLeod would dispute his reasons, and the discussion would turn into a free-for-all. If that happened, Fondilla knew realistically he'd never be able to keep his cool. He'd say things that he would later regret. So he called me in to do it.

I did it easily, with no particular emotional strain, because I had never previously even met my victim. I introduced myself, explained that I was acting on behalf of his boss, who was "too upset" and found it too painful to tell him of his dismissal. I gave McLeod some of the reasons why, and waited for his explosion. His reactions were just what you would have expected. First, he couldn't really believe I was authorized to act on behalf of his boss. Second, when I convinced him I was, McLeod insisted he had to see Fondilla directly, and without me, to ask reconsideration. Of course, I couldn't stop him. I should have realized beforehand that it was the only logical step he could have taken.

So McLeod went in to see the vice-president. They had a thoroughly nasty session, which evolved quite quickly into name-calling and abuse. It accomplished nothing.

How the Consultants See It

McLeod stayed fired, and the vice-president remained upset and angry. (Maybe more so). So Fondilla's little management gambit—using me to do the dirty work—failed. Today, you wouldn't be able to get me to play that role again.

One of the effective management consultants I know is Robert Lull, president of Brooks International Corporation, of Westwood, N. J. This is a company that specializes in solving production and manufacturing problems. Bob told me he thinks one of the most useful things his firm can do is to recommend executive dismissals, where no practical alternative exists.

"We don't work in the executive board room environment," Bob said. "We do our work out on the floor. We're production people. We're installers of systems, not advisors. And often, we see executives in an entirely different light than the top boss sees them. Probably our opinion of executives is much worse, much more critical, than the average person's opinion.

"When you work closely with people for a number of weeks, you get to know them a lot better than the boss who's sitting up there in the office. He's too removed from the real state of affairs on the factory floor. When he wants to know what's going on, he talks to his supervisors and his middle men.

"If they're incompetent, these middle level people try to set up what I call a Fort Bragg inspection of the troops. Everybody shows up for inspection with his shoes shined, if that's what the boss wants. They tell him what he wants to hear.

"Well, we come in with our staff, our troops from the outside, and believe me, we were not summoned to analyze the quality of the shoe polish. Our troops start charging into machine gun fire, tackling the problems. Pretty soon we can observe how the company executives conduct themselves under difficult circumstances. We quickly learn who's who. The excuses they've been giving the top boss often fall apart when wc dig into the problems. These incompetent managers change tremendously when they realize our staff sees through many of their excuses.

"Why are we there in the first place? Because production isn't going right. Or because it's costing too much. We're experts in these things.

"The worker on the production line can't solve the problem. He hasn't got any authority. The foreman has little enough. And so on up the line, until we meet the executive who's in charge of production. Sometimes we find a man who has failed to do *anything*. If he were doing his job, he would long ago have acted on the problems. He should have gotten out there and worked on these problems, and he knows it. That's the job of an executive. Instead, he's done nothing.

"And too often," Bob went on, "the more amazing thing is that the top boss doesn't recognize where the real problem lies. What happens if Bernie, one of the vice-presidents, isn't right for the job? The president may not want to face it. He picked Bernie in the first place. He doesn't want to face the possibility that maybe he made an error in judgment when he gave Bernie the job.

"I see this sort of thing happen frequently. It's difficult for the president to make the hard decision. I remember Angus Connor, a man in a chemical company where we worked recently. I think that was his name. He was good looking, smart, knew his stuff. But he had no stomach for making unpleasant decisions. I simply couldn't convince his boss that he had to go. So I set up a meeting with the president. I had briefed the president beforehand on what questions to ask the man. Sure enough, Connor walked in smooth, self-confident, talking positive. But when the hard questions came, he just melted away. He had never been asked those things before. I practically had to scrape him off the floor and take him back to his own office. The boss was convinced that Angus Connor should be dropped."

If your management has brought in outside consultants to study your area of operations, the best thing you can do is to cooperate with them. They're being paid to produce results, to improve productivity or service, or to cut costs, or whatever. If you help them, they're more likely in turn to help you (or at least not harm you) than the fellow who gets in their way.

Every management consultant has his own stories to tell of frightened and misguided managers who commit hara-kiri by refusing cooperation. Bob Lull told me a typical story. "On an assignment last year," he said, "we were working for the director of manufacturing operations. One plant manager named Paul Cardigan gave us a hard time right from the start. This guy had 600 or 700 people working for him. He was, I suppose, in the $25,000 salary range. He showed pretty obviously that he didn't want us messing around in his plant. It soon became apparent he wouldn't give us the right time of day.

"One of my staff came to him and asked him for studies he had made of his plant operations during the past six months. We knew the studies existed because the director of operations had told us so, and we wanted access to them.

" 'I'm sorry,' Cardigan told me, 'but that is confidential information.' Just imagine his stupidity.

" 'Yes, but you've already been told to cooperate with us and to give us anything we want.'

"The plant manager started getting in deeper. He certainly had a knack for making problems for himself. He told my project chief, 'Yes, I heard that. They told me. But it doesn't apply to these studies because I did them in my personal time. In my opinion, this study is not company business. It's my personal business. But anyway, my answer is no; you can't see them.'

"What a jerk Cardigan was! Right there, we had all we needed to go back to his boss and get him out. But that wasn't enough. We decided to go over the head of this manager and talk to his shift supervisors. The first one we got to said, 'Look, fellows, I'd like to help you out. But Mr. Cardigan says I'm not supposed to help you any more than is absolutely necessary. I'm just supposed to answer questions, not to volunteer information.'

"When that happens, you know right then and there that his supervisors have something they want to tell you. This wasn't what he was supposed to say to us. So my project chief said to the shift supervisor, 'Let's pretend he didn't say that.' And the guy came back and replied, 'Well, if he didn't say it, here's what I would tell you.' And three hours later, my man had the whole story. He found out what was wrong, where the troubles were, and went to work on them immediately."

What this supervisor told the consultant was no "Fort Bragg inspection." It was instead the real story that had been hidden from management by the plant manager. The consultants reported the situation to the boss, which resulted in the manager's dismissal. Without his exit, the problems could never be solved.

Management consultants have a responsibility to their clients. So does the executive to his company. If people don't meet their responsibilities, they have to be either neutralized or removed. It's one thing if a man has done his best, yet hasn't been able to solve the problem. Frequently, such a man should be retained. But it's another thing if he willfully obstructs your management consultants who are trying to solve the problem. That means he doesn't want anyone to find the answer. From my perspective as a management consultant, excuse me for suggesting that such a man deserves dismissal.

11
Mr. Nice Guy

THE STORY OF MY LONGTIME BUSINESS FRIEND, ED McCALLUM, IS THE STORY OF HIS EXCESSIVE RELUCTANCE TO FIRE KEY EMPLOYEES WHO SHOULD HAVE BEEN FIRED A LONG TIME AGO. Ed's experiences forced him to change his mind about corporate executions barely in time to save his business from collapse.

McCallum is the president of an extremely successful service business. He is well respected by his customers and his competitors alike. I know him well enough personally to say with certainty, Ed McCallum is a very decent human being. He has entertained my wife and me in his home, and we have had him in ours. He has always impressed me both with his business success and his absolute self-honesty. Never have I heard him, in the intimacy of a long-standing friendship, attempt to deceive himself as to his shortcomings or his assets.

Ed McCallum was always proud of one thing especially: he never fired any of his key management people. Never. Absolutely never. That used to be his basic tenet of good management.

I asked Ed McCallum if he himself had ever been fired.

"Yes, once, Chet. I was working in the shipping room of a tie factory in New York—Elsa's Cravats. This was right after World War II and I needed the money very badly; I was working my way through college. My base pay then was probably 25¢ or 30¢ an hour, and after about a year, I asked the owner of the shop for a raise of 5¢ an hour. Well, my employer fired me on the spot. He said he could find a replacement for the job at the rate that I had been paid. He was very cost-conscious. There was no personal animosity involved.

"That was the only time I was ever fired. It didn't cause me any suffering; in fact, it was hardly much more than a temporary inconvenience. I remember how elated I was when a few days later, I found another job at 35¢ an hour. That seemed like very big money to me. So that little experience wasn't what shaped my attitudes toward firing. It really happened a long time before that when I was a little boy and saw what poverty had done to my father.

"I can remember incidents that haunt me to this day. I can remember the first time I realized how poor we were. I saw my father cutting out pieces of cardboard to put in the soles of his shoes, because he couldn't afford to have them repaired. I remember him walking out into a drenching rainstorm with these cardboards in his shoes. We lived in Brooklyn then, and my father didn't even have the fare to take the trolley-car over the Williamsburg Bridge to Manhattan to get to work. This is what the Depression did to him. It broke him."

Ed sat back paused, lit his pipe, and puffed deliberately, "You know, Chet, for emotional reasons, I find it very difficult to fire anybody. It used to be that I'd look at an employee's personal situation and extrapolate all the terrible difficulties he would suffer if I were brutal enough to fire him. I let this overwhelm my judgment to the point where I wouldn't act, even if he were totally ineffective.

"I'd think of a man's family burdens. My managers had homes; they had children; they had wives. These were people who did not come from well-to-do family situations. They were people who had moved upward on their own talent. Therefore, they didn't really have any financial reserves. I would empathize greatly with these people. I would place myself in their situation and say, my God, if *I* were fired tomorrow before *I* had accumulated any money, what would happen to Vira and the children?

"My memories of childhood linger. They influence me against taking any action that would put a family in distress. That's the way I regard firing. I think in terms of what it will do to the man's children."

Ed's emphasis on children was interesting from a psychological viewpoint. I suddenly saw that Ed McCallum recalled his childhood experiences not from the perspective of his unemployed father, but from his own viewpoint as a little child during the days of the great Depression.

"I'm frankly embarrassed to admit it to you, but the

truth is that I never once fired an employee—not just my key executives, but anybody—for ten years, despite the fact that many really deserved being fired. Ten years. Ten years!" Ed McCallum shook his head in apologetic embarrassment.

"During those ten years, I lost only one key employee whom I should have fired long before. I lost him because he died of alcoholism in that pathetic ward of Bellevue Hospital. Drink killed him. He had been drinking right along. On two occasions, he cost me valuable customers by showing up in their offices in an inebriated condition. He made a scene, and they promptly cancelled their orders. I still couldn't bring myself to fire him. Why?

"Because six or seven years earlier, before I opened my own business, he had been my boss on one of my first jobs. He had gone out of his way to look after me and some of the other youngsters on his staff. I couldn't forget that.

"If I, or one of the other young men made a real error, he would take the blame himself. He'd say to *his* boss, 'Sorry, I goofed.' His boss knew it was a lie. But he was a decent human being, and he was doing this for all his young people.

"Now he had really become an alcoholic, and every time he made problems as my employee, I'd call him in to discuss dismissal. His hands would begin to shake, and he would slump down in his seat. And I'd recall that he was a bachelor, with no family; no one to take care of him. I'd have memories of how, when I was in my mid-twenties, he had saved my job when I made errors. So I couldn't bring myself to fire him.

"It was a real problem for me, because I couldn't afford to keep a non-productive person. The business was too young and shaky in those days. I needed to apply every dollar toward a productive person. But one Monday morning, I came back from vacation and was told that he had died of the D.T.'s. On my payroll to the very end!

"There was no one to claim his body. No one to pay his funeral expenses. So I did that too. Found the name of the little town in Arkansas he had come from and arranged with the pastor of the country church to give him a decent Christian burial.

"So you see why I'm a bad example to talk about firing. He was the only man that ever 'left me' during those ten years. And not because I fired him but because he killed himself with drink. You'd have to admit that's an extreme example of my ineffectiveness in this area.

"Then there was the case of Herbert J. Neal. I even made some personal sacrifice for him. I reduced my own income because I knew of his own economic needs.

"One of the reasons I'm so angry at Herb now is that he would come to me very frequently, sometimes after I had just given him a healthy raise, and say, 'I need more money because my wife is spending like crazy.'

"And I would say, 'That's not our firm's role in life, to provide your wife with all the spending money she needs.' He once told me if he made $1,000,000 she would spend $1,000,000 and that's true. When economic conditions forced me to cut salaries, we cut his minimally.

"I took a larger proportionate cut than anyone else to make up for his smaller reduction. That's one of the reasons I'm resentful of his reaction. When he left my company for another job, his comment hurt like hell. He said, 'I owe you nothing. I owe your firm nothing. I owe none of the other people in this firm anything. The only ones I owe anything to are my family.'

"Now perhaps he's correct; I don't know. But I said to him, 'I sacrificed a great deal over the years to give you increasing income at times when you didn't deserve it, just because your wife was spending again. I thought there was some loyalty due back to the firm.' I got none.

"I'll tell you another experience that convinced me that I was being taken advantage of. When I finally had to fire one of our younger men, he said to me, 'I wonder why you hadn't fired me a half a year ago. I never really put in a full day or did the work I should have done.'

"I told him that I was aware that he hadn't, but he had so much potential that I hoped that I could nurture him to the point where he would be effective for us. Keeping him was a conscious decision on my part. It was not my inability to fire him but my desire to invest in him. When he left, it never bothered him that he had given me no return on my investment.

"Some of the employees I kept the longest because their need was the greatest turned out to be most ungrateful. The unkindness. For instance, Dave McDavid is no longer with us. You don't know him, so let me describe him. He weighs pretty close to 350 pounds. He's mammoth. He is not attractive.

"Dave was running into severe financial problems. He couldn't find a job; his clothing was becoming tattered. At that time, we needed an employee. I took him in until he could get a permanent spot. He ended up staying on and as the firm grew, he performed good services.

"But one day, Dave put me in a very awkward spot. Since we were doing so very well, his salary was quite good. He said to me that he had finally decided to build the house of his dreams. And he had bought a very large property in Fairfield County and was putting up a $100,000 house. But he had no collateral. Would I co-sign for him?

"I explained to him that I couldn't possibly co-sign a $100,000 note for his house. It was not a burden I cared to take on. And his response was 'Well, I've already told the bank that you would do this. You're a millionaire. I'll be wiped out if you don't co-sign and I'll lose this property. Can't you do this for me?' So I did.

"When the recession hit us, we had to cut everybody's salary and when we cut Dave's salary as well, he could not make his payments to the bank. He then came to me and said, 'You know, I can't make it. You've got to give me more money.' Instead of taking a reduction, he wanted a $10,000 raise above the salary that he was getting then. And I said, 'Dave, knowing our position at the moment, you know this is impractical.'

"So after a couple of months, he came in and said, 'I've found another position.' And he went to work for another firm. I was a damn fool. I'm stuck with $40,000 of the amount that I co-signed for. I can't get out of this one. Is there any way to make a recovery? Not unless I put him in bankruptcy and take his house away from him, which I wouldn't do."

"Ed," I commented, "You've been decent, kind and human as a boss. You've done this both for rational reasons, and as a result of your childhood conditioning.

"Now you're saying that after all this experience, you've discovered that your kindness was not really appreciated. The financial generosity you showed meant nothing. Are you also saying it's better to be tough?"

Ed McCallum replied, "Yes. I'm saying that I wish I had been a bastard. I can appreciate for the first time the bosses who are tough and who seem to show no regard for their employees. People like my friend Jim Doswell. I don't know if you know Jim.

"He's always told me that I'm an imbecile to treat employees the way I do. He's the extreme other end of the scale. As far as he's concerned, they're nothing but chop meat. Jim says I'm absolutely stupid to maintain any per-

Mr. Nice Guy

sonal feelings of concern. Nobody cares about you when the chips are down, he says. You are alone. He feels that people are to be used for his own personal gain for as much as he can get out of them. Pay them as little as possible. Work them as hard as possible. When they're not useful, dismiss them. Keep them in a constant state of fear. 'Fear raises productivity.' he says. I don't know that it does. I think it reduces quality of performance.

"This past year, I changed a lot of my own philosophy regarding personnel. I formerly believed that a company president's job was to orchestrate the ambitions and fantasies of his employees so that one not only reached the corporate objectives and goals but permitted the employees to believe that they were also achieving their own aspirations. This past year, I discovered that an old Goldwynism is true. Sam Goldwyn once said, 'Every time I find a nobody and make his a somebody, he ends up thinking I'm a nobody and I have to fire him and find another nobody to make a somebody.'

"I still find it emotionally difficult to fire. But now I've insulated myself from my employees. I will not permit myself to get emotionally involved. I don't want to know anything about their families; I don't want to know about them other than the quality of their work. And I will probably have a hatchet man, which is a disgraceful thing, I think, to have in any firm. But I can't fire people myself."

"If a guy needs to be fired," I asked Ed, "and psychologically it is too damned difficult and upsetting for you to do, what's wrong with getting somebody to do it for you?"

"I think that it is dishonorable for a man to put another human being in the role of being the corporate bastard. I feel that to be the president of an organization, one must be emotionally equipped to do the dirty work as well as the creative planning and thinking. My attitude toward people gives me trouble. I don't feel that I ever have the right to humiliate another person, to denigrate him, reduce him as a human being. I don't think that employees are to be subjugated. I don't think I own a man because I pay him a salary. I think I rent his services; no more than that. And he's to be treated with respect."

"It firing disrespectful to him?"

"As you see, that's my problem. I suppose that's why I need a hatchet man, but I feel guilty about it.

"You can see clearly, Chet, what caused my problem. Not only my childhood memories, but my temperament. I want to be liked. I think anyone who goes into a business dealing with other human beings wants to be liked, seeks the approbation of other people. Well, my motivation and drive built the business. But my need to be liked almost wrecked it.

"Probably the firm would have been healthier if I had fired people sooner and if I had had a hatchet man to do it for me. I did fire people only under extreme economic duress. It was a most emotional, jarring thing. Now I will no longer hesitate. But I won't do it myself, because I can't bring myself to do it. Who will do it? I'll appoint someone in the firm even though I think it's improper of me."

It's just possible that the candidate for hatchet man will welcome the post psychologically. The "right" man might relish the opportunity to crack the whip and be the company son-of-a-bitch. If Ed removed from him the responsibility for making the decision, and left him only to carry it out, he might be a happy head-chopper indeed, totally freed of personal guilt.

Ed McCallum—Mr. Nice Guy to his staff—is Mr. Nice Guy no longer. He learned at painful cost that dismissals may be cruel in their consequence, but failure to dismiss may lead to even worse results.

12
Should You Give it Another Try?

WHEN YOU THINK OF THE POSSIBLE CONSEQUENCES OF YOUR DISMISSAL ACTION, YOU MAY BEGIN TO WONDER WHETHER YOU SHOULDN'T GIVE THE MAN A FEW MONTHS MORE. The experience of Ed McCallum is only one reason why you shouldn't. Your own instincts are an even better guide.

After all, when you hired him as a manager, you trusted your instincts over-and-above all the tests and references and interviews. Now, if your instincts tell you he isn't making it, I think you should follow those instincts.

Telling him if he doesn't improve he'll have to leave in six months is a mistake, because he'll be unable to function with your sword poised over his head.

Keeping an executive on the job six months after you've decided he's failing is no favor to him. It's only going to hurt him more. Six months from now, more damage will have been done to your company. He will be six months older and perhaps six months less employable for that reason. You'll be six months angrier at him for having failed to perform what he is unable to do. And six months from now, the job market may be worse so that he'll have a harder time, not an easier time, getting relocated.

Have mercy.

Do it now.

Otherwise, ten years from now, one of your successors will be saying, "Why didn't someone fire that man ten years ago?"

There is really no way that you can make a dismissal pleasant. You can make it only painful instead of shatteringly destructive. You can minimize the man's embarrassment in front of his friends and colleagues. But you can't make it into an enjoyable experience, and you're deceiving yourself if you think you can.

Is there anything worse for a man than the act of dismissal? Is there anything more destructive to a man's self-esteem than to tell him he has failed? Indeed, the larger the company or department from which he is being dropped, the greater his sense of failure because he knows that he has been singled out from all his working associates as the one who is not up to their standards. He knows that firing means that he has failed. Is there any easy way to absorb that painful information?

Nor is there a way that will enable you to keep the person's friendship at the end of the firing session, because what you've really said to him is, "I don't love you anymore!" That's the way the dismissed manager hears it, and there's nothing you can do to change that.

Nevertheless, there are practical as well as psychological reasons for trying to make the rite as painless as possible. For instance, the man you're firing may know some of your valuable trade secrets. Even if they're less valuable than the top-secret formula for Coca-Cola or Worcestershire Sauce, he may have, for example, vital facts on how your company assembles its automatic control devices. In some companies, as many as one-third of the employees have some knowledge of trade secrets, according to a recent study made by the Conference Board, Inc.

You can warn the terminated executive of his continuing legal responsibility for protecting those formulas—most companies do. But it's just common sense that if he walks out of your office seething with hostility, he might very well blabber valuable information that should be protected.

So abide by common sense instead of the law, and try to minimize his hostility. There are practical ways you can dismiss a man without adding insult to injury.

Pick your timing carefully. "I try to avoid firing anyone just before Christmas, because it once was done to me," says Joseph Sanchez. "In my first job, on Christmas day, my firm sent out telegrams to a number of people, including me, saying, 'Don't come back to work. We'll send you what ever personal items are in your desk.' Apparently, they had to reduce the staff by the end of the year, but there must have been a better way. On the other hand, that was the time when fewest number of people were on hand. Virtually everybody was off, so that made it easier for management."

You'd think Christmas is the worst possible time for

a dismissal, but as Mr. Sanchez points out, management clearly had considered the timing and didn't agree. The Christmas period can be a disaster to the company that selects it for head-chopping, in my opinion.

In any case, you'll need to consider not only the month, but the day of the week and even your setting to avoid additional embarrassment to your victim. If people are passing your office door constantly, then better close it so you'll be able to talk without the danger of being overheard by other staff members. Don't let the man leave your office in a state of shock just at the moment when his associates are passing by on their way to lunch.

Another business friend of mine says, "Don't tell 'em what I go through. I'm known as a Tiger in this company. I'd rather they keep thinking that." [Name withheld] says, "Even if the man deserves it, I always find myself feeling sorry for him. That's an impossible situation for me. How can I dismiss him if I feel guilty? So I try to get myself all worked up about how he deserves it, and how he's really no good at all. How he's an ungrateful so-and-so. If I can make myself feel angry at him, and show it on my face the next morning, I hope it will be much easier to do what has to be done. But I never can be sure." He fears it.

So do you. But finally, after all your evaluation, meditation, consideration, reconsideration, consultation, procrastination, reflection, cogitation and contemplation, you've reached a decision: the man must go.

It's now no longer "if" but "how." Having made your mind up, you're ready to act. Now. Immediately.

But don't move rashly. You've still got a few steps to go. You must assure yourself that the man's departure doesn't leave a vacuum. Whatever he's been doing, his work must be well covered. You need a successor for the man you'll be terminating.

Should You Give It Another Try?

A second step is to analyze possible damage to your company's position.

Barney Jacobsen, a longtime friend of mine, has this responsibility in a sales department. I won't identify his company here for obvious reasons. Before Barney's boss fires a salesman, Barney develops a written battle plan to contact the company's customers before the dismissed salesman can reach his key accounts and try to take them with him to his next employer. Barney showed me one of his plans. It was stamped on the cover "Company Secret" (the corporation's highest security classification). It listed the man's major accounts, when he last called on each (the information taken from his own sales records), whether any immediate orders were pending, the nature of the salesman's relationships (for instance, whether the customer was merely his occasional luncheon companion, or whether they had ever golfed together, etc.), and whether any other member of the sales organization knew the customer personally and could therefore be used to notify him of the dismissal.

In this company, and departing from the usual Friday-afternoon timing, dismissals from the sales force were always made early in the week so the company could reach key customers promptly. For the same reason, lunch-hour timing was avoided. If the sales manager called in the man to give him the news, say at 10 o'clock on Wednesday morning, you could be sure that at the same moment in three other offices, three other officials, often including Barney himself, would be telephoning the victim's three major customers. And when a personal visit instead of merely a phone call was deemed prudent, you can be sure that at 10:15 a.m. sharp, a company official would be walking down Lombard Street or St. Paul Place to visit those customers. Barney minimized damage to customer

Walking the Executive Plank

relations. His management is convinced it's worth the effort.

If you've finally decided the time is at hand to face the ordeal of firing, nothing can fully prepare you. Conrad Sauchelli, a hotel manager, says that after having dismissed not less than 75 or 100 people during his career, he still feels his stomach muscles tightening and his neck muscles tensing when he knows the time has come for a termination interview. He dreads it.

Be prepared for emotional outbursts, tears, wrath, or whatever. They may happen despite your calmest manner. Be human and try to understand. If necessary, you might even give the man a word of consolation and comfort. Don't criticize or ridicule him for showing his emotion. Better for it to come out in the privacy of your office than after he gets out in the corridor and makes an awkward and painful scene.

Whether you've decided to tell the man the exact reasons for your action, or merely mention them in vague generalities, (as discussed in Chapter VII) you should have firmly decided long before the man entered your office. You should know what you want to tell him. Some managers pencil their key points on a card for reference during the interview.

Ed Cassell, a public relations supervisor here in New York, tells me that at home the night before, he'll actually write out a rough script of what he wants to say to the man he's going to dismiss. He reads it aloud a couple of times to make sure he has said all that he wants to say and none of the things he doesn't want to say. Then he tries out his little drama on his wife; she plays the part of the employee and starts arguing. Ed says that between the two of them, they're usually able to anticipate what's likely to happen

Should You Give It Another Try?

on the morrow, and to prepare him for it. He doesn't relish it.

It's usually better to break the news just as soon as the man has entered your office and sat down. Don't lead up to it. Give the bad news directly, and then spend the rest of the time softening the blow and letting the impact sink in. You might say, as an opening sentence, "Malcolm, I'm sorry to have to tell you this, but we've decided to terminate your services as of this afternoon."

Don't get emotional. Keep your tone of voice low. Speak slowly. Moderate your volume. If you talk to the victim in an angry tone, he'll respond in kind.

Most important, avoid the word "fire." Any euphemism is better. In a big paper company headquartered in the South, formal written instructions to executives read: "The word 'firing' has an unhealthy connotation. Its use is not permitted. It is better to say, 'relieved of duty' or terminated.'"

Whatever words you use, it's a useful device to remind the man that others who haven't been successful with your company have nevertheless gone to other firms and done very well. You might point out that it's not just a question of how well he performed, but how well his performance met the needs of the company, and this latter might have been beyond his control.

Don't pass the buck. Don't blame someone else for the firing decision unless there are special reasons why you should. Don't blame "management;" you're management. If you are carrying out a decision you didn't make and don't agree with, better to say nothing as to who made the decision than to excuse yourself.

"I once had to notify a close friend of mine that he was fired," J. G. Randall, a Newark division manager told me.

"I told my boss I didn't think the decision was right, but if he wanted it done, I would do it. I called in my friend immediately and told him he had the choice of resigning or being fired on the spot.

"Right away, he knew it wasn't me. It's just not my style to call people in out of the blue and say, 'You're fired.' My friend knew instantly what had happened; that the decision hadn't come from me. But I never said a word about that. I simply said a decision had been reached by management. I suggested that we work out a reasonable settlement that would compensate him fairly, and avoid any fireworks or rash actions. And we did work something out."

There's a piece of Texas humor I've heard that seems appropriate here. According to the folklore, a hospitalized man is told that his heart is failing and he's going to need a transplant. The doctor tells him he has three hearts to choose from—all from men deceased that very day. One man was a young athlete killed in an auto accident. The second was a school teacher. The third was a personnel director. "I'll take the personnel director," says the man. "I want to be sure I'll get a heart that's never been used."

In defense of the supposedly heartless personnel director, however, let me say that the ones I know are just as human and considerate as any corporate line manager. But years of involvement in personnel matters have given them a hard protective covering. They have learned how to do things like firings without emotional involvement, simply because that's the only way they can survive professionally. I know one personnel director who just before he came to lunch with me fired a vice-president. (He had told me about his plan beforehand.) Over a drink, I asked him how it went. "What went?" he responded. Fifteen minutes later, it had already been dismissed from his mind.

He wasn't the slightest bit discomforted when I commented on the fact.

This emotional detachment is fine for the personnel director. It's fine for anyone who has to do firings frequently. But it's terrible for the victim, because it leaves him with a feeling of the "ruthless and heartless corporation" at a time when he desperately wants some expression of human sympathy.

That's primarily why you should consider doing the firing yourself, instead of asking a personnel man to do it for you. In terms of your interests and the company's this is one occasion where a little warmth is more desirable than a clinically cold encounter. If you happen to be a personnel director, I suggest you resist the "opportunity" to become the corporate executioner. There are better uses for your professional skills.

"When I got fired from the company," Louis Berger (no relation of mine: we spell our names differently), a lower-level supervisor told me, "the personnel man did it. I practically saw icicles on his upper lip. The man was smiling. What was so funny about it? It was my job lost, not his. He was reading from a memo in front of him, but when I asked him for a copy, he said he couldn't give it to me. The whole thing, the way he did it, was quite infuriating." That's not the way to do it.

I've known of cases where dismissed management executives asked as their last request if they could please participate in writing the staff announcement of their departure. Some, fearing loss of face, made a big thing out of the exact wording, ". . . resigned . . . his new plans will be announced shortly . . ." or ". . . has decided to leave us to take an important new post soon to be revealed . . ." Frankly, I don't think the words of the announcement are important one way or another. After all, even the mail boy learns to break through the polite screen of concealment and to recognize that these memos are notifications of dismissal. Euphemisms avoid embarrassment for all concerned. If such an announcement isn't made to the staff, however, the rumor mill will begin to grind, and it's been known to happen that the Departed One immediately comes under suspicion of all sort of evil malpractices.

To avoid such damaging rumors, I'm perfectly willing to let a man write the text of his own memo unless he is being terminated for cause. I suggested to one company that at the time they terminate an executive, they show him the draft of the proposed memo, and allow him right then and there, to modify it if he wishes.

You should show human understanding and sympathy for the man. At the same time, you should have a realistic understanding that the man's continued employment will endanger the jobs of others. Assuming there are honest and reasonable grounds for his dismissal, this is literally true, and not a glib rationalization.

For a company is an organization, a team, and there is a close relationship among all the performers. The sales manager who, by ineptitude, fails to sell the products being manufactured; the production manager who fails to produce sufficient product to fill orders promptly; the financial officer who fails to keep the company in a liquid condition, endangers not only his own job, but the economic survival of the company, and therefore everyone else's job too.

The philosophy of management is that the organization must be served. I have heard young people say that this is precisely what's wrong with the capitalist system, that profits come before people. But in my corporate lifetime, I have seen many examples pointing in precisely the opposite direction. I've seen executives who weren't doing their jobs (and often weren't even trying to do their jobs) kept on the payroll until they dragged down the morale of everyone in their organization. Their colleagues reactions were, "Joe isn't working and management doesn't bother him. So why should we work?" In such an atmosphere, I have seen whole departments and even whole companies fail, unable to keep with their competitors.

I am convinced that a requirement to perform well brings out the best of people's abilities. Or, to put it another way, when "security" is made more important than "performance," job security is endangered rather than protected. Look at the dreary drudgery of Post Office jobs, or at teaching jobs in public school systems. The government, as an employer, has put "security" first. There are minimal performance standards to be met. There are only civil service jobs to be protected. Incompetence permeates the tenure-protected ranks. No one can get fired. (Theoretically, it's possible, but just try it!) You can't help but wonder whether rank-and-file employees, customers, students and the public alike wouldn't have been better served if incompetent managers in those organizations had been stripped of their tenure and fired years ago.

It isn't pleasant to see once-motivated and able men turned into time-servers, their enthusiasm and self-respect destroyed out of a misguided desire to protect their management jobs. I know of one fellow who was a good man in the wrong job. Instead of quitting, he made a conscious decision not to look elsewhere. "I just go along, do what I'm told, and keep my nose clean," was his philosophy.

Of course a capable supervisor soon spotted his lack of performance and fired him. Afterwards, he came to me and said, "I wasted three years of my life. Now I have to look for a job anyway. I didn't avoid anything. But I'm three years older." That's not the way to live your life.

So, assuming there are valid and objective grounds

for a man's dismissal, I believe you do him, in the long run, a service by severing him from the organization. The corporate world, particularly at the upper management levels, is full of presidents and vice-presidents who have achieved greater triumphs after being fired from jobs elsewhere.

You may even want to help the man find a new job. Not by concealing the fact of his dismissal, not by trying to unload him on an unsuspecting friend in another department or company, but by helping him in an honest way to get a new position elsewhere.

One high corporate executive tells me that he'll go to considerable efforts to help a dismissed employee get a new job if he's convinced that although the man was unable to perform effectively in a particular situation or personal relationship, he's qualified for something elsewhere and is well motivated.

"I have the opinion," he says, "that a lot of any job is your attitude, your feeling, the 'chemistry' with your boss. The interaction of people is important in any company. I know of many situations where a moderate performer became a star performer when we changed his boss. Also, we often have an opposite situation: a good performer suddenly gets bad ratings because he has a new boss. If we have to fire a man like that—and sometimes we do—I think he's entitled to any help I can give him."

I asked him how he went about helping.

"I'll call a few business associates I know who may be looking for people," he said. "And I'll tell them honestly that I just fired a man they might be interested in hiring. I always describe these people accurately. I never over-endorse them. I don't think you should ever do this. It's not fair to the individual you're trying to help, because his new employer's expectations will be too high. It's better to be absolutely honest, not only to protect yourself and your company, but also the other employer, and even the man himself."

It all adds up to this: if you're convinced that the man isn't doing the job you want done, terminate him. Do it carefully. Do it at the right time. Do it when it won't injure your company. Do it as kindly as you know how. Help the man get a new job if possible. Don't embarrass the man.

But let him go before someone screams, "Uncle."